TIM HAWKINS

TOTALLY

TRANSFORMED

Totally Transformed
© Tim Hawkins/The Good Book Company 2010

The Good Book Company
Tel: 0845-225-0880; International: +44 (0) 208 942 0880
Email: admin@thegoodbook.co.uk
Websites:
UK: www.thegoodbook.co.uk
N America: www.thegoodbook.com
Australia: www.thegoodbook.com.au
New Zealand: www.thegoodbook.co.nz

Hawkins Ministry Resources
PO Box 7569, Baulkham Hills Business Centre,
NSW, 2155 Australia; Fax: (+61 2) 9629 6595
E-mail: info@hawkinsministry.com
Website: www.hawkinsministry.com

ISBN: 9781907377358

Design: Steve Devane
Printed in the UK

CONTENTS

SECTION

1

TOTALLY

TRANSFORMED

ME

I want to feel new!

I love getting things that are new! There's nothing quite like a brand new mobile phone, a brand new hairstyle, a brand new computer, a brand new boyfriend or girlfriend, or a brand new... whatever.

I remember my first car. It was a 1959 VW Beetle. Okay—it was 13 years old when I bought it, but it was new for me! I loved it. I washed it. I polished it. I degreased the engine. I painted red stripes on the tyres to make it go faster. You couldn't get me out of it!

But there's a problem with new things. They don't stay new for long. And very soon, no matter how many techno-gadgets you end up with, there comes a point in your life that every teenager dreads. This is the one feeling that you do not want ever to experience. This is a painful pit that you do not want to fall into.

"I'm bored!"

Aarrgghh!! There it is! The enemy of vibrant youthfulness. The assassin of magical dreams. The destroyer of positive futures. Boredom!

my first car!

7

THE PROBLEM OF TELLING YOUR MUM

You know how it goes. It's getting towards the end of the school year. You're counting down the days when that school bell will ring for the last time. You're getting close to that long summer holiday break—where you can be released from the tedium of the classroom to enjoy all the world has to offer.

Finally the holidays arrive! Freedom at last! No more school uniform. No more teachers. No more books. Lots of lovely sleep-ins with unlimited time to do anything you want!

This is so fantastic! This is what you've dreamed of for so long. And it's all going brilliantly—for the first few days—and then you run out of things to do… your friends have all gone away… and then you painfully realise… *"I'm bored!"* And if that wasn't bad enough, you then do the one thing that you've been warned **never** to do when you're bored around the house **— you tell your mum!**

Oh my goodness! How could you? Because as soon as tell your mum that you're bored, she will unleash two of the most destructive weapons that she has at her disposal…

Tidy that room!

1. She'll find things for you to do

"Mum, I'm bored!"

"Well, if you're really bored, then there's plenty to do around here. Why don't you tidy your room, or mow the lawns, or help me clean the kitchen, or stack the dishwasher, or sweep the paths, or wash the windows, or help with the gardening, or do the ironing, or clean the toilets, or put out the rubbish, or…?"

Could it get any worse?

"And when you've done all that, you could get a head start by reading your English novels for next year!" **Aarrgghh!!**

All these things are great and noble things, and you might have the nicest mum in the business, but this is not the answer to your boredom! C'mon, you want to do something good—you want to do something exciting—you want to do something new!

"But mum, I'm still bored!"

Now that's an incredibly dangerous thing to say! Because it's then your mum brings out her most horrific, soul-destroying weapon...

2. She'll take you shopping

"Well, you're not going to be bored any longer. You can come with me to the supermarket."

Aarrgghh!!

The supermarket with mum! The shopping trip from hell! You know you're going to take hours and hours wandering up and down every single aisle, looking at every single product and comparing expiry dates, buying boring things like brussel sprouts and toilet cleaner, and not going anywhere near the interesting aisles.

Aarrgghh!!

You know what it's like when you go shopping with your mum.

"Oh look—they've got undies on special! Stand still so I can see whether they'd fit you!"

Then she ropes in an innocent passer-by:

"Do you think these would fit my daughter? She's a little bit chubby in the derriere!"

I need to add a little footnote here. My wife is a lovely lady. But for the sake of our marriage we have agreed that we don't go shopping together. Or to be more honest—for the sake of our marriage *I* have agreed that we don't go to the supermarket together! We just shop in such completely different ways!

If I'm going shopping, I know what I'm after, I find it, I check the price, I buy it and I'm out of there. A lot of blokes shop like that. It's the hunting instinct. You hunt it, you shoot it, you bag it and you're gone.

Some women I know seem to enjoy the **experience** of shopping. Taking their time, looking at everything. And this is all fine for them. But I go out of my mind if I'm with them!

IT'S SOMETIMES HARD TO FEEL NEW

No-one wants to be bored. Most of us want things to be new and exciting and different and transformed. You don't want the same old food; you don't want the same old family holiday at the same old holiday house; you don't want the same old clothes; and you don't want the same old, boring books.

New hair...feel great!

Things that are new have an excitement about them. The first camp you went on. Your first overseas holiday. Your first rock concert. Your first date. Your first kiss.

One of the real tragedies is that I know that for many teenagers—they don't feel very new at all. They don't feel transformed. They don't feel different.

Somehow being a teenager is meant to be fun and carefree and new and exciting. People will tell you: **"My teenage years were the best years of my life!"** And you can look around you and honestly feel: **"If these are the best years of my life, I'm in deep trouble!"**

It's so easy to feel that things aren't going very well. On the outside you can fool people by looking cool, calm and confident, but deep down it is far murkier. I have met many precious teenagers who don't feel very good about themselves at all.

I know some girls who look at themselves in the mirror and all they see is someone who is very fat. They're not fat at all, and even if they were, what does it matter? They are beautiful, young women, but they look at themselves and they don't like what they see.

I know some guys who look in the mirror and they desperately want to be taller and stronger, and all they see is someone who's a bit puny. And rather than seeing the fantastic person that they are, they just see someone who's little and weak.

And you want to know that you're developing normally—you want to know that sexually you're growing on track—and if you can't see it, you can get really down about yourself.

It's so easy to feel lousy about yourself. It always seems you're not as clever as you want to be, or you're not as good looking, or you're not as popular, or you're not as rich, or you're not as cool, or as smart, or as strong, or as developed; you're not sexy enough, suave enough, successful enough...

You can look deep down at yourself and see all your faults, and basically feel *yuck*. You can be the most popular kid at school, and still feel lousy inside. And I know that this is going on for many of you—day in, day out.

Every now and again,
you just say "stuff it"

IT CAN BE HARD TO FEEL NEW AS A CHRISTIAN

And whether you feel good about yourself or lousy about yourself, sometimes it's hard to feel excited about living as a Christian.

Sure, you know it's all true, and you know deep down that you want to follow Jesus, but sometimes it's just plain hard work to live his way. You know you've got to follow God, but you don't feel like doing it. You hate having to obey him; so every now and again, you just say: *"Stuff it"*, and you start living in ways that you know bring huge dishonour to the name of Jesus.

There are things you might be doing. There are people that you may have hurt.

But whatever your situation, I know that God has something powerful to say to you right now. I know that God wants to talk with you about one of his favourite topics: **you!** There are some incredible things about yourself that God wants to tell you.

> ### 2 Corinthians 5:17
> *Therefore, if anyone is in Christ, he is a new creation;*
> *the old has gone, the new has come!*

If you've become a Christian, that means **God has made you to be a brand new person,** and he's designed a new and exciting life for you to lead. He has totally transformed you!

Do you believe that? Do you believe that God has something new and powerful to say to you as you read this book? Well, fasten your seat belts and hang on tight. I want to look at a section of the Bible where God talks about you. Yes—you! **A totally transformed you.**

We suggest you read on...

2 God has transformed me!

Let's check out some of the great stuff that God has already done for everyone who has become a Christian!

Ephesians 1:3
Praise be to the God and Father of our Lord Jesus Christ, who has blessed us in the heavenly realms with every spiritual blessing in Christ.

Do you like getting new things? Do you like getting lots of presents? Me? I love Christmas! Christmas is such a great time of year. Yes, it's weird, we sing songs in front of a dead tree and eat chocolates out of our socks… but it's great!

Can you remember as a little kid, waking up early on Christmas morning, and badgering mum and dad to let you open your presents? Maybe you had a pillowcase that "Santa" used to fill up with all sorts of goodies, and you had so many presents that you hardly knew what to do with them?

Ephesians 1:3 says that every spiritual blessing—or if you like, every spiritual present— that God the Father could give you he has **already** showered on you! **You've already got it!** Look again at Ephesians 1:3:

It's 3am, can we open our presents now mum?

"God ... has blessed you in the heavenly realms with every spiritual blessing".

Everything you need to be a brand new person in Christ—he has already given it to you! Everything you need to be a totally transformed person—he has already given it to you!

Maybe there are some presents God has given you that you haven't got to yet. Maybe there are some you're a bit scared to unwrap. Perhaps there are some spiritual blessings that you don't understand and don't know what to do with. Or maybe there are some presents from God which you haven't even found yet!

But this verse says that God has already given them to you! And the rest of the letter to the Ephesians is a celebration of all the great spiritual blessings that God has poured out on every person who is in Christ. Ephesians is like a "Santa sack" of spiritual blessings that makes you totally transformed if you are indeed a true Christian. It is the instruction manual so that you know how to live in a way that enjoys every new gift from God.

We're going to have fun in this book unwrapping these presents. More importantly, God is going to show you how to live as his faithful person in a few really tricky areas. **More about that later!**

Right now I want to show you five of these fantastic spiritual blessings that God has already given to every person in the world who is a real Christian.

1. ELECTION – I AM CHOSEN BY GOD

Ephesians 1:4
For he chose us in him before the creation of the world to be holy and blameless in his sight.

This is the first massive gift from God that makes you absolutely special and absolutely brand new: **God chose you.** Now, you might be thinking "Didn't I choose God?" Yes, you did, but the Bible says you can only choose God if he first chose you! Listen to Jesus' words:

John 15:16

You did not choose me, but I chose you...

John 6:44

No one can come to me unless the Father who sent me draws him...

What a fantastic spiritual blessing! It wasn't just up to me to make my own decision to follow Jesus. God had already chosen me to be his!

You may not fully understand what all this means (I don't!), but let's look at what we can understand. Here are two important questions:

a) When did God choose you?

Look again at the same verse from Ephesians:

Ephesians 1:4

For he chose us in him before the creation of the world...

Is that mind-blowing or what? If you know for certain that you are a follower of Jesus, try saying these words to yourself—out loud!

"God chose me before the creation of the world!"

Are you starting to wrap your brain around that? Okay, let's now look at a second question:

b) What did God chose you to be?

Look again at the same verse:

Ephesians 1:4

For he chose us in him before the creation of the world to be holy and blameless in his sight.

That's how God sees you. *"Holy and blameless"*. You are **holy.** Special— set apart to be his child. And you are **blameless.** God doesn't hold a single thing against you!

If you belong to Jesus, there is the first great spiritual blessing from God that can totally transform you—God chose you!

Here's the second one!

Next verse:

Ephesians 1:5a
In love he predestined us...

Here's the second great blessing or present from God. The second reason that you can know that you are special. The second reason why you can know for sure that you've been made absolutely brand new— **God has predestined you.**

Now predestination is one of those words that are really easy to get hung-up about. But it is a very simple concept and we experience it every day. Predestination simply means that you give something or someone a destination—before the journey has started.

Imagine you want to catch a train or a bus to somewhere special. When the train or the bus comes in, how do you know if it is the right one? How do you know where it will end up on its journey?

Simple, really! There's a destination sign on the bus or train that tells you where it's going!

Final destination

Now, here's the tricky question. When was that destination sign put on the bus or train? Did the driver put it on half-way along the journey? No! The destination was all decided on long before that train or bus started its journey!

That's what predestination means. It means that you give something or someone a destination **before the journey has started.**

That's what God has done for you! If you belong to Jesus,

then that means that God has decided on a destination for you long before you even started your journey here on planet earth!

So—what is the destiny or destination that God has already given to you?

3. ADOPTION – I AM GOD'S CHILD

Ephesians 1:5
In love he predestined us to be adopted as his sons through Jesus Christ…

Here is the third great spiritual blessing. The third present from God that makes you very special— makes you absolutely brand new—makes you totally transformed. Not only did God choose you, but also he predestined you to be adopted as his child.

I don't know if you know much about adoption. Perhaps you've been adopted yourself. Maybe you know someone who's been adopted or who has taken on an adopted child.

He makes us into his own children

You can understand the principle of adoption if you've ever bought a pet for your family. Let's imagine that you've all decided that your family should have a pet rabbit. You've gone down to the pet shop—you've selected your rabbit—you've taken him home. That bunny rabbit is now part of your family. He will now enjoy all the privileges of being in your family. He will now experience all the love that your family has to offer.

Can you see the enormous privilege of having the king of heaven adopt you into his own family? God doesn't just call you to be a slave, not even just a friend, but he calls you to be his own precious son or daughter. You get to call God dad!

God has chosen you; he has predestined you; so he can adopt you as his child.

Now you need to understand that God's adoption is very different from the way we adopt. Let's go back to the story where you adopted your pet rabbit. If you were down at the pet store, how would you go about choosing the one which would be yours?

> *"Aaaaaah! Look at that cute, little white one—he's got gorgeous, big eyes."*

> *"Yes, he looks great! But I don't like that one next to him. Look—he's scratching all the other poor little bunnies!"*

> He takes people who are his hardened enemies—he takes people who deserve his condemnation and punishment—and makes them his own children

Is that the way God adopted you? Did he choose you because you were the prettiest, or the strongest, or the smartest, or the best behaved? No! God did not adopt you that way. God doesn't adopt anyone that way. He takes people who are his hardened enemies—he takes people who deserve his condemnation and punishment—and makes them his own children.

Romans 5:10 (paraphrased)
We were God's enemies, but he made us his friends through the death of his Son…

That's right. God doesn't adopt us because *we* are fantastic— **he adopts us because *he* is fantastic!** Look at how he describes choosing his Old Testament people—the nation of Israel.

Deuteronomy 7:7-8
The LORD did not set his affection on you and choose you because you were more numerous than other peoples, for you were the fewest of all peoples. But it was because the LORD loved you and kept the oath he swore to your forefathers that he brought you out with a mighty hand and redeemed you from the land of slavery, from the power of Pharaoh king of Egypt.

Can you imagine God choosing someone who is sinning against him—someone who is his enemy—and adopting them into his own family and loving them as his own precious child? And yet that's what God has done with every one of us who belong to Jesus!

Imagine that after you've taken your rabbit home to be your own special pet, some neighbourhood kid breaks in and attacks your pet bunny. He steals your bunny—skins him alive—kills him and then stuffs the rabbit's guts into the lasagne that you're baking in the oven. When you take the lasagne out of the oven, you see those little bunny eyes looking up at you…

Oh! That's horrible! Stop it! That's outrageous!

Let's imagine something even more outrageous. When the police catch that kid who's tortured and killed your rabbit, imagine that your parents decide to adopt that kid into your family! They treat him with a love as great as they give to you. They give him as many presents as they would give to you. And they write him into their will so that this kid gets just as much inheritance as you do!

That's outrageous!

But that's exactly what God does every time he takes one of his enemies and makes them into his child. That's what he's done for me. And if you belong to Jesus, that's what he's done for you!

So how is God able to take his enemies—deserving his punishment—and bring them into his own kingdom as precious sons and daughters?

Blessing number four!

God doesn't adopt us because we are fantastic, he adopts us because he is fantastic!

4. REDEMPTION – I HAVE BEEN BOUGHT WITH A PRICE

Ephesians 1:7

In him we have redemption through his blood...

Okay—another tricky word. Redemption simply means that you buy something back with a price. The word comes out of the slave market that operated in those times. If you borrowed money, and you couldn't pay it back, then you were taken into slavery by the person you owed money to. You became their slave for the rest of your life! The only way out was if somebody paid everything you owed—then you could be released from slavery. The person who paid your debt and bought your freedom is said to have **redeemed** you.

Redemption always means two things:

a) The thing you pay for is set free.

b) There is always a price you have to pay.

Imagine that you're enjoying your favourite games arcade. Where there's all sorts of machines you can put money into—and all sorts of games you can play. Have you ever played at one of those old-fashioned places where you win a series of tickets every time you compete? The better you do in the game, then the more tickets you get. When you have enough tickets, you can redeem them for prizes which are kept in a display cabinet.

That's what redemption means. All those fluffy little toys are being kept imprisoned by the evil arcade owner—and displayed to the entire world in his glass cabinet. All their freedom taken away. Never to be released.

Until you redeem them. You pay the price. You win the victory on the game. You set the little furry creatures free.

Remember? Redemption always means two things:

a) The thing you pay for is set free.

b) There is always a price you have to pay.

That's what Jesus has done for us. We were held captive in Satan's prison—chained down by our own sins and guilt. And yet Jesus made the ultimate sacrifice—he paid the ultimate price—when he offered his own life to set us free.

That's the fourth great blessing from God. Through Jesus, he redeems us!

It costs

Ephesians 1:7

In him we have redemption through his blood, the forgiveness of sins ...

I find it hard to think that I could possibly have all this from God because I know I've done some pretty bad things. And maybe when you look around you, it doesn't seem real for you either. You might not feel as good as all those super spiritual, Bible-believing, boldly witnessing, disciple-making, morally pure champion Christians that you're surrounded by.

Can anyone set me free?

You look around at everybody else and you know you could never be as good as them.

Because deep down, it's easy to feel that you've failed. You know those sins that are deeply personal, and you know that you'd die of shame if anyone else found out. It's so easy to think:

"How could God love someone like me, who has let him down so often?"

That's the joy of blessing number five from God. Forgiveness. If you truly belong to Christ, that means he has absolutely forgiven you for every wrong thing you could possibly do. (More about that in Chapter 20!)

So if you really are a totally transformed person, there's something really important that you now need to do. (Next chapter!)

3

I've got a whole new way to live!

If you've stayed with us for the last two chapters, you will have discovered some amazing things. Can you now see that if you are truly following Jesus, you are indeed a brand new person? You have been totally transformed!

And because God has given you his Spirit to live in you, he keeps on making you to be a brand new person—every time you are forgiven! Of course, you might be thinking:

> *"I don't know if God has totally transformed me. I don't know if I really am forgiven. I'm not even sure I'm genuine about being a Christian."*

That's okay. This book is the perfect place for you to hassle all that through—at your own pace. By the time you get to the end, I think you'll have worked all that out.

But if you really are a totally transformed person, then there's something really important that you now need to do.

2 Corinthians 5:17

Therefore, if anyone is in Christ, he is a new creation; the old has gone, the new has come!

What does God mean: *"the old has gone, the new has come"?*

Imagine that you're home by yourself, and you hear a knock at the front door. When you open the door, you're absolutely amazed! It's Jesus! Imagine that! Jesus has come to visit you!

"Are you going to let me in?"

"Sure thing—come on in!"

Jesus comes in and asks:

"May I see your room?"

"What, my room?"

"Yes! I want to see your bedroom!"

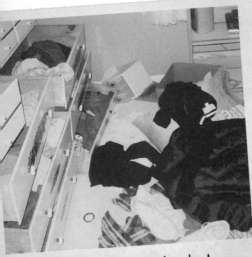

If I knew You were going to do this, I'd never have invited You in!

Oh my goodness! Your heart is starting to pound. Thousands of thoughts are racing through your head.

"Maybe I shouldn't have put those posters up on my wall! Perhaps I should have tidied up! I hope he doesn't check the "history" tab on my internet browser!"

But there is Jesus standing in your bedroom.

"Are you going to get me a cup of tea?"

"Of course—right away!"

While you're down in the kitchen, you hear the most amazing racket! It's the sound of furniture being trashed—you hear things being dumped and broken. You race back and Jesus is throwing all your furniture out on the front lawn! He's trashing the place! He's ripping down all your posters. He's clawing the wallpaper off the wall. He's going through the house and throwing out all the furniture! He's dumping the TV and the sound system and the computer and the fridge—oh my goodness—what will your parents say when they get back?

You finally yell out:

"Jesus, what are you doing?"

But he holds up his hand to silence you.

"Jesus, if I knew you were going to make such a mess, I would never have invited you in! I just wanted a pleasant cup of tea with you! I didn't expect you to start a major demolition project!"

And when Jesus has thrown out absolutely everything you own, then you see him directing in a huge van,

New for old — not a bad deal

and there's a team of workers bringing brand new gear into your house. Everything top quality. Everything better than what you used to have. There's a giant 3D plasma TV screen. The latest computers. Really modern furniture. Brand new carpet. Everything!

You see, when you ask Jesus into your life, sometimes you only want a quiet cup of tea with him. You want to live life with no changes whatsoever. But what you don't realise is that when Jesus takes over your life, he's going to perform an *Extreme Makeover.* And it's not just the surface paint and furnishings he's going to change. He's going to transform you deep down inside. He's going to turf out everything that has no place in a totally transformed person's life—and replace it with quality stuff that reflects his glory.

Yes, coming to Jesus will cause some pain. There'll be stuff in your life that you want to hang on to. There will be things that you need to give up. But the only reason that Jesus wants you to get rid of that stuff is that he's got something far better that he wants to replace it with! If God has made you into a totally transformed person, then he now gives you a brand new, totally transformed life to live!

If you want to live a totally transformed life, there is a very important step you need to take—which has two parts:

GET RID OF THE OLD PUT ON THE NEW

2 Corinthians 5:17
Therefore, if anyone is in Christ, he is a new creation; the old has gone, the new has come!

This verse says that when you're a brand new person—something important must happen: *"The old has gone; the new has come"*. Before you can put on God's brand new way of living—you've got to get rid of the old ways!

It's like coming home after having a mud-fight with the neighbourhood kids.

Manky

Your clothes are trashed and stinking. In fact, they're so utterly, absolutely filthy they can never be made clean again. They're only fit for the trash.

Your mum meets you at the door and barks out an order:

"Go upstairs and put on some clean clothes."

You do what your mum says—you put on some clean clothes. But when you come downstairs, your mum yells at you again!

*"I meant for you to **take your old clothes off** before you put your clean clothes on!"*

You can't just take brand new clothes and put them on top of your old filthy, stinking, decaying clothes! It doesn't work! First you have to take off your old clothes and throw them away!

In the same way, you can't just take the new ways of living that Jesus wants for you and put them straight on top of your old ways of living! You're meant to throw away your old, sinful ways of living! Get rid of them completely! Have nothing more to do with them. Then you can really live the new way that God wants you to.

One of my problems is that I like to hang on to my "old clothes"—my old sinful ways—and put them in the back of my spiritual wardrobe, "just in case". Sometimes I slip them on under my new clothes. Sometimes I wear them instead of my new clothes.

It's so easy to hang on to your old sinful way of living—and it's so easy to go back to it any time you want to. If you're struggling with pornography—don't leave the old magazines lying around your room—chuck them out! If you're listening to illegally downloaded music—don't leave the CDs on the shelf or tucked away on your hard drive. Destroy them! Erase them!

No wonder so many people find it hard to live the brand new life that Jesus has for them. Maybe you're still playing around with your old life. Maybe there are things that you need to get rid of—right now.

The Bible puts it this way:

Ephesians 4:22-24
Everything—and I do mean everything—connected with that old way of life has to go. It's rotten through and through. Get rid of it! And then take on an entirely new way of life—a God-fashioned life, a life renewed from the inside and working itself into your conduct as God accurately reproduces his character in you. ("The Message" Bible Translation)

Sometimes it's really hard. I know many of you struggle with it—and I know some of you are really trying. And if you fall flat on your face from time to time—hey, God understands that—and he's not there waiting to condemn you for anything.

In this book I want to help you with the five most difficult areas where so many young people struggle to live a totally transformed life. If you want to jump to a particular topic right away, then do it now. You don't have to read the rest of the book in order. You can go to the section that best deals with the issues where you're finding it a struggle.

1. What I say? *Totally Transformed Speech*

Do you struggle with your words? Do you put others down with angry words? Are you trapped in the habit of swear words? Do you find yourself using dirty words? Come and learn how your whole way of speech can be totally transformed so that you will inspire others with your words of life. **Page 33**

2. How do I deal with parties & alcohol? *Totally Transformed Fun*

Sometimes the hardest place to be a Christian is at a party. How do you deal with the issues of alcohol and drugs? How can you learn to have genuine fun in a way that doesn't compromise your principles?

Page 63

3. How do I cope with my parents?
Totally Transformed Submission

The real test of how you're going in living a life of totally transformed submission is how you're going with your own parents. Both Christian and non-Christian parents bring their challenges! How can you reflect the values of Jesus in the way you treat your folks? **Page 89**

4. What is God's plan for my relationships?
Totally Transformed Sex

This is the big one for Christians to think through. When it looks like everyone else has abandoned the Christian values for sex, how do you stand strong for Jesus in a way that means you will get the best out of your sexuality? **Page 115**

5. How should I live with my non-Christian friends? *Totally Transformed Mission*

Sometimes the areas of greatest temptation are when you're hanging out with your non-Christian mates. How can you be active in reaching your friends without falling into their low standards? **Page 141**

And of course, there's a big conclusion for everyone—**on Page 163**—don't miss it!

God has made you a totally transformed person. This week—will you start to live a totally transformed life?

TOTALLY

TRANSFORMED

SPEECH

4 Your most powerful weapon

Have you ever imagined how great it would be if you were given one magical ability that would give you supernatural powers?
As a kid, did you ever dream of finding a magic wand or a magic genie that could somehow give you a special power over everyone else? If you could have one special power—what would you like it to be?

THE SILENT HORDES

They found the Professor sitting in front of his auto-screen

And in your more evil moments… have you ever wanted the ability to cut someone else down to size, to take away their superiority and just crush them beneath your feet? Come on, admit it! At some stage in your life, you have probably secretly wanted to snuff someone else out and turn them into a puppy dog that would just beg at your feet!

That wicked primary-school teacher who always made fun of you in front of the other children. That pesky brother or sister that always gets you into trouble. That guy who took your girl away from you (or vice-versa!).

Or maybe you dream of having the ability to give life and strength and hope to others?

Someone you care about is really down—someone you love is hurting—wouldn't it be great if you had the ability to make things work for them? Wouldn't it be brilliant to somehow give them the power to be the person that God has designed them to be

GOD HAS GIVEN IT TO YOU!

Here's the good news for you today: **God has already given you something powerful which can give genuine life and hope to other people.** And he has also given you the ability, if you use this power the wrong way, to destroy others and rob them of the future that they're longing for.

Right now, go and find a mirror. Yes—a mirror—and take this book with you. Strand in front of the mirror so you can see your whole face—close up. Right now I want you to discover one of the most powerful weapons that God has placed right within you. On the count of three… one, two, three…

Poke out your tongue!

leeuuw!

YOUR TONGUE

Your tongue—this is the powerful weapon that God has given you which you can use to build other people up—or tear them down. This is the powerful weapon that God has given you which can speak words of life—or speak words of death.

When you become a Christian, God remakes you as a totally transformed person. Everything about you is made new. Right now I want to show you from the Bible that your **speech** has been made new. Your speech has been totally transformed. God has something fantastic in mind for your speech, for your words, your tongue.

God wants to remake and renew your tongue and use it in a way that is going to be an amazing blessing for so many others.

Are you ready?

a) Your tongue is powerful

It can change lives!

I love the way the American preacher, Charles Swindoll, describes the tongue:

Like a bit in a horse's mouth...

> *To the physician, the tongue is merely a two-ounce slab of mucous membrane, enclosing a complex array of muscles and nerves, that enables our body to chew, taste and swallow. It is also the major organ of communication that enables us to articulate distinct sounds so that we can understand each other … Without the tongue no mother could sing her baby to sleep tonight. No ambassador could adequately represent our nation. No teacher could stretch the mind of students. No officer could lead his fighting men in battle. No attorney could defend the truth in court. No pastor could comfort troubled souls. No complicated, controversial issue could ever be discussed and solved. Our entire world would be reduced to grunts and shrugs.*

Our tongue is certainly important! But on top of everything else—it can change lives!

James 3:3-4
When we put bits into the mouths of horses to make them obey us, we can turn the whole animal. Or take ships as an example. Although they are so large and are driven by strong winds, they are steered by a very small rudder wherever the pilot wants to go.

Imagine how big and powerful a horse is. Way stronger than any human. And yet when you're riding a horse, you have complete control as to where this mighty beast goes because of the tiny

... or a rudder on a ship

bit that you put in its mouth. Your tongue—although a small part of your body—is powerful like that.

Or think of a ship on the ocean. Perhaps a giant aircraft carrier. How do you control the direction of such a mighty ship? By the small rudder placed at the rear. Your tongue—although a small part of your body—is powerful like that.

It's like your whole big TV set being controlled by one itty-bitty remote control. Whoever has possession of that remote control has the position of power within the family. One pesky little brother or sister who changes the channel while you're watching your favourite show can ignite World War 3 in your family!

James 3:5
Likewise the tongue is a small part of the body, but it makes great boasts.

Do you understand the power of your tongue? Like the bit in a horse's mouth… like a little rudder on a big ship… your tongue—though it is small—has the ability to turn other people's lives right around and head them in the right direction.

Proverbs 18:21
The tongue has the power of life and death

When I left school, I had no real idea of what I was meant to do. I certainly had no concept of what **God** was preparing me for. I settled for a salesman's job in a retail store—I was happy enough, but there was no real direction in what I was doing. Certainly, I wasn't changing anyone's life!

And yet, after I had been plodding away in retail for four years, three separate people spoke words of life into me. None of these three people knew each other; their words to me were totally disconnected, but I received three different messages in the one week. These three different messages all said the same thing: **"Tim—I think you should go into youth ministry!"**

Ever wanted to hit "rewind" after you've said something?

Those words were the catalyst for a huge change in my life. Shortly afterwards I left work, went to Bible college, and started life as a youth pastor. Over thirty years later, and I'm still doing it! Powerful words indeed. Imagine that those people had not spoken those words of life into me. If they had kept silent, you would not be reading this book now!

Your tongue is amazingly powerful. Although it is one of the smallest parts of your body, it is one of the most potent weapons that God has given you. You can literally change the direction of someone's life!

b) Your tongue is dangerous

It can destroy lives!

> ### James 3:5-8
> *Likewise the tongue is a small part of the body, but it makes great boasts. Consider what a great forest is set on fire by a small spark. The tongue also is a fire, a world of evil among the parts of the body. It corrupts the whole person, sets the whole course of his life on fire, and is itself set on fire by hell. All kinds of animals, birds, reptiles and creatures of the sea are being tamed and have been tamed by man, but no man can tame the tongue. It is a restless evil, full of deadly poison.*

Words can destroy so quickly. And once you have said them, words can never be taken back. Haven't you ever wanted to hit the "rewind" button after you've said something that you shouldn't? Don't you secretly wish you had a **control-alt-delete** system for your mouth so you could completely eliminate the words you have just said which have hurt someone you love?

You know that things that other people have said to you have hurt you. It might have happened years ago—it might have happened this morning. People have probably crushed you with a hurtful word. You know the effect it has on you.

One morning at church I was standing with a family who had a teenage boy, aged around 15. He was a great hockey player, and I knew that he had just been picked to represent his state. What an honour! I also knew that his dad wasn't very encouraging to him. So I thought I would give the dad an easy opportunity to speak words of life into his son.

"I hear that Michael has been selected to represent his state at hockey!" I said in proud tones. This was intentional. Both the dad and the son were standing right in front of me. This was the perfect opportunity for dad to encourage his son. Unfortunately, he replied: **"Well, it's the first thing that he's ever got right in his whole life!"**

> God wants to totally transform your words and use them in a way that is going to be an amazing blessing for so many others.

Words of death. That's the problem with your tongue. It can change lives. It can also destroy lives. And you know how devastated you feel when you are doing something for a friend, and they never thank you or encourage you. You know how easily you can feel crushed when someone puts you down.

Here's the good news—God has something fantastic in mind for your speech. God wants to remake your words. God wants you to get rid of ways of talking that tear others down. God wants to renew your tongue. God wants to totally transform your words and use them in a way that is going to be an amazing blessing for so many others.

Wouldn't it be great to know that your words were being used by God to build others up and strengthen and inspire them to be the people that God wants them to be?

So how do I avoid these words of death? **Read on!**

Words that tear down

What's the secret to having my speech totally transformed by God?

Ephesians 4:29 [1]
Do not let any unwholesome talk come out of your mouths, but only what is helpful for building others up according to their needs, that it may benefit those who listen.

If we could put this as a filter across our mouths, our speech could be totally transformed. If we could put this as a filter across our mouths, our relationships could be totally transformed. If we could put this as a filter across our mouths, our family life, our church, our nation and our world could be totally transformed. Let's check it out!

Words can kill

UNWHOLESOME WORDS

Ephesians 4:29
Do not let any unwholesome talk come out of your mouths …

Unwholesome —that's a weird word! It's not one of those words that you use every day. "My goodness, you're looking unwholesome today!"

In fact, this is the only place in the whole Bible where this word is translated

---

1 If you've already read *Awesome on the Inside*, you have already been introduced to this verse. But so many people have asked me to explain it further that I have decided to "go deep" with it over the next two chapters!

as unwholesome. The original word describes a bad tree that produces bad fruit. [2] The same word can be used to describe fish that have gone off. [3] Yuck!

But the whole idea of unwholesome means something that is not whole—something that is not building anyone up—something that is not helpful. When something is unwholesome, it always tears away from what it is meant to be.

Wholesome always builds up —it makes you whole… it makes you the way you are meant to be. Unwholesome always tears down… it always makes you less whole—it takes you away from being the way you are meant to be.

It's like food. There is wholesome food and unwholesome food. Now here's the problem—unwholesome food often looks attractive! Full of yummy fat and sugar!

But here's where it gets messy: if that's all that is in your diet, you will be one sick puppy! Try having a total diet of Coke and chocolate bars! It might look tasty, but because it is unwholesome, you will not end up very healthy at all!

Wholesome is good. Filling your car with petrol is wholesome. Filling your car with Dr Peppers is unwholesome. Washing your boxer shorts in laundry detergent is wholesome. Washing them in thick starch is unwholesome—not to mention remarkably uncomfortable!

Unwholesome words can also look attractive. You feel good because you've put down someone else. You've come up with the quick one-liner that makes them look stupid and has everyone else laughing at your quick wit.

"Your mum wears army boots!"

Okay—I realise that no one actually says that, but do you get the point? The quick put-down, while being funny, is actually unwholesome—that is, it tears the other person down.

---

2 Matthew 7:17-18, 12:23 and Luke 6:43—the word for "bad" in "bad tree" or "bad fruit" is the same word that Ephesians 4:29 translates as "unwholesome".

3 Matthew 13:48—the word for "bad" in describing "bad fish" is the same word that Ephesians 4:29 translates as "unwholesome".

Imagine that we all took this phrase from the Bible seriously.

Tasty, but deadly

Ephesians 4:29
Do not let any unwholesome talk come out of your mouths…

Imagine if each one of us made that decision—that no matter what anyone else did, we would make sure that no unwholesome talk was ever going to come out of our mouths! What a change that would make.

And that is a decision that you could take right now!

As we read through the verses in Ephesians that surround this verse, we get an idea of four of the most deadly, unwholesome words that can really mess up our relationships.

1. LYING WORDS

Ephesians 4:25
Therefore each of you must put off falsehood and speak truthfully to his neighbour, for we are all members of one body.

You know how easy it is to say words which aren't exactly true. It's simple to exaggerate things to make yourself look better. It's so tempting to make up an excuse to avoid getting into trouble. Oh—when I think of the variety of lies I used to tell to explain why I didn't have my homework done! Often our first instinct to protect ourselves… is to lie!

If you want to have your speech totally transformed by God, often the first step is to get rid of lying words.

Now—look carefully at Ephesians 4:25 again. **What is the reason given as to why we should get rid of lying words?**

Ephesians 4:25

Therefore each of you must put off falsehood and speak truthfully to his neighbour, for we are all members of one body.

God calls on us to be truthful to each other because we all belong to the same body. It makes sense, doesn't it? Parts of your own body don't lie to each other, do they?

Imagine you are walking along a track, and your eye sees a large snake ahead. What does your eye do with that information? Does your eye think to itself: "Yes, I can see a snake ahead—but hey—I'm an eye—I'm almost two metres off the ground—snakes can't jump that high—I'm safe. I'm not going to tell the rest of the body—they can look after themselves."

Does your body act that way? Mine doesn't! Because my eye is part of my body, it will not lie to other parts of my body. It won't act just to protect itself. It will act to protect the whole body. If my eye saw a snake, it would say: "Danger! I've spotted a snake ahead! Legs—get moving in the other direction! We've got to protect the whole body!"

That's the way your body works. Parts of your body do not lie to other parts of your body because they all belong to the same body. In the same way, as Christians we all belong to the one body, so we must get rid of any words where we lie to each other.

2. ANGRY WORDS

Ephesians 4:31a

Get rid of all bitterness, rage and anger...

Angry words. You know what it's like when you're angry and you're mouthing off at everyone. When you're out of control. Shouting abusive words in the heat of the moment.

It's okay to feel angry. It's okay to be angry. We should be angry at the same things that God gets angry at. We should show anger the same way Jesus did. The New American Standard Bible translates Ephesians 4:26 this way:

> Be angry, and yet do not sin…

So there's nothing wrong with anger, but it's not okay to attack people with hurtful, angry words. The Message Bible puts Ephesians 4:26 this way:

> Go ahead and be angry. You do well to be angry—but don't use your anger as fuel for revenge…

Unwholesome anger can take on many forms. It can be a straight-out attack. Or it can be a slow-burning resentment. **It's still anger.** You know how sometimes you will give your parents the silent treatment? You won't answer their questions. You reply in monosyllabic grunts. You shut them out for hours… or days. That's anger. That's unwholesome. That tears away at your relationships. These are the words that God is telling you to get rid of.

3. GOSSIPING WORDS

Ephesians 4:31b
Get rid of … brawling and slander, along with every form of malice.

Angry words are like straight-out war. But slander and gossip—they're like a terrorist attack that just sneaks up and assassinates people's characters without them even realising it was you. Gossip is when you talk *about* a person rather than talking *to* that person.

"… she's a cheat"

Listen to these descriptions of gossip from the Book of Proverbs:

Proverbs 16:28
A perverse man stirs up dissension, and a gossip separates close friends.

Proverbs 18:8

The words of a gossip are like choice morsels; they go down to a man's inmost parts.

Proverbs 20:19

A gossip betrays a confidence; so avoid a man who talks too much.

Proverbs 26:20

Without wood a fire goes out; without gossip a quarrel dies down.

Gossip is when you talk **about** a person rather than talking **to** that person:

"Did you hear that Marty got drunk at that party?"

Maybe Marty did get drunk at the party. Maybe he needs someone to walk alongside him to help him deal with that in the future. But what he doesn't need is someone gossiping about it. Gossip ruins reputations. Gossip destroys people's good names. Gossip tears apart the family of God. Gossip plays into the devil's hands. Absolutely unwholesome. No wonder God says: "Get rid of it!"

4. DIRTY WORDS

Dirty words

Ephesians 5:4

Nor should there be obscenity, foolish talk or coarse joking, which are out of place, but rather thanksgiving.

You know what obscenity is. Smutty words. Swear words. Foul words. Filthy words. Trash talk. Suggestive words. Words that degrade God's beautiful gift of sex. Words which turn a member of the opposite sex into a sexual object. Words which offend common standards of decency.

Here's the problem: when you become a Christian—when you are totally remade by Jesus—sometimes the dirty words are never cleaned up.

We have lots of camps in our youth group. They are fantastic times of building each other up in Christ. As the excitement of the day carries on, sometimes it is hard to get students to quieten down at night. Often—even after lights out—there will still be noise coming from some of the cabins. Often, I will walk around to help these noisy cabins quieten down.

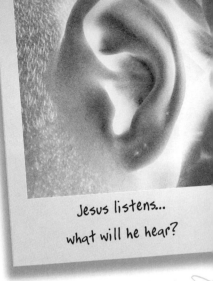

Jesus listens... what will he hear?

Sometimes I will stand outside a cabin waiting to see whether it is wise for me to intervene. Sometimes as I am listening, our young people—our good and godly young people—unaware that I am standing right outside—will continue telling dirty jokes and using foul language. There is always an interesting reaction when they eventually realise I am standing there—hearing everything. There is a moment of high embarrassment. Usually it goes very quiet.

But Jesus is there listening to your conversation all the time! You might not be aware that he's there, but he is. His Spirit lives in you to guide and empower you. The decision to become a Christian is a decision to walk with Jesus for eternity.

As Jesus listens to your language, what will he hear? Is it possible that he will hear unwholesome words? Might he hear lying words… gossiping words… angry words… dirty words?

Do you struggle with this sometimes? Here's the good news—God has not left you alone! He has empowered you with his Spirit so that everything is made new—including your speech.

But how do I speak that new speech? Next chapter!

6 Words that build up

Okay, God has shown us what sort of speech to get
***rid** of, but what are we meant to replace it with?*
The second part of Ephesians 4:29 has four key steps
*to follow—four questions you can ask of **anything***
you're thinking of saying.

Ephesians 4:29
Do not let any unwholesome talk come out of your mouths…
1. *but only what is helpful…*
2. *for building others up…*
3. *according to their needs…*
4. *that it may benefit those who listen.*

Let's check out these four key steps to having our speech totally transformed.

1. BUT ONLY WHAT IS HELPFUL

This is the first key phrase. Here is a question you can ask of anything you want to say to someone— **will it help them?**

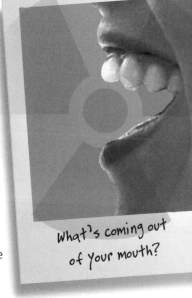

What's coming out of your mouth?

Sometimes we say things merely to help ourselves. To make us look better. To make us sound smarter. To make us feel good. What if we got rid of all that and determined that we would only say something **if it helped the other person?**

There's the first thing to ask of anything you are about to say to someone:
Will it help them? If it will genuinely help them—then say it! But if it won't help them—then don't say it!

2. FOR BUILDING OTHERS UP

Every word you say will either tear others down or build others up. One of our problems is—we often don't want to build others up. We want to build ourselves up. We think that if we put others down, we'll look better.

But your own body doesn't grow like that. If your big toe is feeling a little undervalued, it doesn't start complaining that your mouth is getting all the attention. If your belly-button is feeling a little overlooked and is concerned that your hands get to do so many more things, it doesn't launch a plan to spread gossip about your hands and undermine them. As Christians we all belong to the one body—it's okay to build other people up. Because when you build others up— **everyone benefits!** But guess what? When you tear other people down— **everyone loses!**

Imagine you were committed to deliberately and intentionally building others up. Wouldn't it be great to know that others really got ahead with their life —and really started flying as a Christian—because you were the one that took the time and the energy to build them up? Imagine what your youth group could be if all of us were dedicated to building each other up, not to tearing each other down!

Because there is a warning in Scripture about what a Christian group will become if they keep tearing each other down:

> **Galatians 5:15**
> If you keep on biting and devouring each other, watch out or you will be destroyed by each other.

There's the second question you can ask of anything you want to say to someone— **will it build them up?** If it will genuinely build them up—then say it! But if it won't build them up—then don't say it!

3. ACCORDING TO THEIR NEEDS

Here's the third question you can ask of anything you're wanting to say to someone— **do they need to hear this?** Please note—this can be a different question from **do I need to say it?** Sometimes you might need to **say** something, but the other person might not need to **hear** it!

Subject: i'm really angry!

ow could you do that! I mean its not as though you
is really stupid and be must be a woir-d

Let's imagine you're annoyed with someone. Something they've done has really ticked you off. You have steam blowing out your ears. There's a whole lot of stuff that you simply have to get off your chest. Do you have some things you need to say? Absolutely! **Does the other person need to hear this?** *Maybe not!*

If you have some things you really have to say to someone, try writing it as a letter. Or type it as an email. **But do not type in their email address! You don't want to accidentally send this before you have thought about it!** Anyway—write it all out—say **exactly** what you want to say—and say **everything** that you want to say. When you've finished—read it all through again and make sure it's said the way you want it to be said. **Then sit on it for 24 hours. *Do not send it. Do not show it to anyone.* Sit on it!**

You have now said what you want to say. So ask the third key question— **do they need to hear it?** Often you will find the answer is "no". You might work out that if the other person heard it, it would destroy your relationship with them. Or it might hurt them badly. Or it might discourage them so much that they might give up.

If they don't need to hear it—don't send it. Don't keep it. Destroy it! You've now got it off your chest and you haven't done any damage to your relationship. If of course you work out that they **do** need to hear it—then still don't send it. Catch up with them for a cup of coffee where the two of you can talk

Talk to them — face to face

heart to heart. If you have something negative to say about a person, don't put it in print. Don't tweet it. Talk to them face to face so that you can resolve it.

There's the third question you can ask of anything you want to say to someone— **do they need to hear this?** If they genuinely need to hear it—then say it! But if it they **don't** need to hear it—then don't say it!

4. THAT IT MAY BENEFIT THOSE WHO LISTEN

You've got to be convinced that the other person will benefit by what you say.

There's the fourth question you can ask of anything you're wanting to say to someone— **will they benefit by hearing this?** If they will genuinely benefit—then say it! But if it they **won't** benefit at all—then don't say it!

Let's just double check the guidelines that we've seen from Ephesians 4:29— the five checkpoints that we've outlined over the last two chapters.

THE OVERALL GUIDELINE

Do not let any unwholesome talk come out of your mouths…

Imagine if you did nothing else except to make sure that no more unwholesome talk came out of your mouth—no more lying words, no more angry words, no more gossiping words, no more dirty words. Can you imagine the difference that would make to your life? The difference it would make to your family? The difference it would make to everyone you met?

Now add on to this guideline the four questions you will ask of anything you are planning to say to anyone:

1. **Will it help them?**
2. **Will it build them up?**
3. **Do they need to hear this?**
4. **Will they benefit by hearing this?**

Imagine that no parent would ever speak to their child unless their speech followed all those guidelines. Imagine that no teenager would ever speak to their parents unless they put these filters over their mouth. Imagine a school, or a youth group, or a church, or a community where **everyone** was committed to speaking words of life!

Don't wait for anyone else! You can start this yourself—today!

Words that encourage

Words sometimes get a bad reputation. "It's just words. Meaningless words. Anyone can say something nice. It doesn't mean anything!"

In part, I agree. Sometimes we can use words, and not mean them at all. When the shop assistant says to me: **"Have a nice day",** I don't really mind—at least they're being polite. But I don't **really** think that they're concerned about my well-being! I think they are saying **mere words.**

Your call is REALLY important to us

Yeah — right

I hate it when I ring up and I find that I'm talking to a computer robot. Eventually after an endless round of **"Press 1 for customer enquiries..."** I end up hearing those dreaded words: **"Your call is important to us. We have placed you on priority."** Priority? Is that what they call it? If my call was **really** important to them, they wouldn't have me talking with some stupid robot— **they would give me a real human being to talk to!**

55

Words are never meant to be empty words.

Ephesians 5:6

Let no one deceive you with empty words…

REAL WORDS BRING REAL CHANGE

As you read through Paul's letter to the Ephesians, you see that genuine words will bring a genuine change.

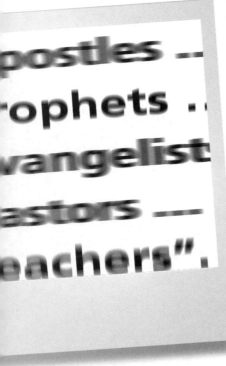

Ephesians 4:11-12

It was he who gave some to be apostles, some to be prophets, some to be evangelists, and some to be pastors and teachers, to prepare God's people for works of service, so that the body of Christ may be built up…

God has a plan to grow his people. And his plan starts with words. He gives ministry gifts to everyone, and to some he gives the "word" gifts. God enables some people to be able to use words to reach and strengthen those around them. In the verses above, there are five key ministry gifts which God says he will use **"to prepare God's people for works of service, so that the body of Christ may be built up".**

So, which five ministries does he identify as being capable of preparing other people for service? *"Apostles … prophets … evangelists … pastors … teachers."* There you have it. And without going into what **precisely** each one of these terms mean, can you spot the similarity? **All of them are ministries that use words to change the lives of others!**

Real words are meant to bring real change.

Ephesians 5:19

Speak to one another with psalms, hymns and spiritual songs …

That means the way we speak to each other really matters. We are to take God's word and speak it to each other. We are to build others up and help shape their lives by the way we speak to them.

Words are never meant to be empty. They are always meant to change lives. If God's word is really at work in your life, then you will…

Apostles ..
Prophets ...
Evangelists
Pastors ....
Teachers".

Ephesians 4:22-24

put off your old self … to be made new in the attitude of your minds, and … to put on the new self, created to be like God…

If the word of God really has taken hold in your life, then you will **"be imitators of God … and live a life of love …"** (Ephesians 5:1-2).

GENUINE ENCOURAGEMENT UNLEASHES OTHERS FOR MINISTRY

One of the greatest ministries you can have is that of encouragement. Encouragement is simply when you recognise other people's strengths, tell them what they're doing that's good, and inspire them to achieve more with what is possible.

You could be the person who builds up another and enables them to have an awesome ministry! Who, me? Yes—you!

Think of a time when someone else encouraged you. They pointed out something good that you'd just done—or a helpful attitude that you were displaying. Didn't you feel great? And didn't it inspire you to keep doing that more and more? As God develops you to have totally transformed speech, let's learn together the steps to be a genuine encourager.

The song that you played was fantastic!

Come on—if you want to be critical, you'll always see something you can criticise. But if you want to be an encourager—you'll always be able to see something you can praise. That's why God keeps working at changing your heart. Because it's what's in your heart that will control what you see. And what you see will control what you say.

THREE STEPS TO BEING A CHAMPION ENCOURAGER [1]

Step 1: "Just then..."

The first step in encouraging someone is to make a simple observation about something good that they've just done.

> *"Just then, the song that you played was fantastic."*

> *"Just then, you did a great job of cleaning up after our youth group night."*

You don't have to use the phrase **"just then".** It's just to help you to remember it. I have used it in the two examples above to emphasise it.

If you did nothing else except Step 1—and did it constantly and consistently with everyone—you would be such a blessing to all those around you. But

---

1 These steps are so important that I even teach them to business leaders! You can find a "business" version of "How to encourage" in *Every Leader's SmartBook*

encouragement reaches a new height when you go to the next level:

Step 2: "Right now..."

This is where you give **your reaction** to the good thing that the person has done:

Thanks for clearing up mate!

> *"Just then, the song that you played was fantastic." (Step 1)*

> *"When you play like that, right now I am inspired to praise God more and more!" (Step 2)*

> *"Just then, you did a great job of cleaning up after our youth group night." (Step 1)*

> *"Right now I feel so encouraged that you put so much effort in." (Step 2)*

One again, you don't have to use the phrase **"right now"**. It's just to help you to remember it. I have used it in the two examples above to emphasise it.

This is the step that **builds relationship.** By giving your personal reaction to the other person, you are drawing them into a closer relationship with you. This is inspirational stuff!

Step 3: "One day..."

This is where you look to the future. You get to be a little bit prophetic. This is where you inspire someone else to greater heights. This is where you attempt to answer this question: **"If this person keeps showing this positive attitude, what might they achieve?"**

> *"Just then, the song that you played was fantastic." (Step 1)*

> *"When you play like that, right now I am inspired to praise God more and more!" (Step 2)*

> *"One day, if you keep playing like that, you will encourage thousands of people!" (Step 3)*

"Just then, you did a great job of cleaning up after our youth group night." (Step 1)

"Right now, I feel so encouraged that you put so much effort in." (Step 2)

"If you keep showing that attitude, then one day, God will use you in a really big way." (Step 3)

Can I give you some homework? I want you to intentionally practise those three steps of encouragement. **This week** can you make sure that you:

- **encourage every single member of your family?**
- **encourage someone at school?**
- **encourage a leader at your church?**

Go on—you can do it!

TOTALLY TRANSFORMED SPEECH

Proverbs 18:21
The tongue has the power of life and death...

Everything you say will be a word of life or a word of death. Everything you say will either push people down or raise people up. Everything you say will give away what your heart is really like.

If you are in Christ, you are a new creation. If you are in Christ, God has totally transformed you. Remember that everything you need to be a brand new person in Christ—God has already given it to you.

Imagine what it would be like if your speech was totally transformed as from today! Imagine the difference it would make if you stopped speaking words of death, and focused on speaking words of life. Imagine what it would be like if your whole youth group became a community which did not let unwholesome talk come out of their mouths. But we all spoke only what was helpful—for building others up—according to their needs—so that it would benefit all who listened.

If you are a Christian, God has totally transformed you. If you are a Christian, God has totally transformed your speech. Every time you open your mouth from this point onwards… will you tear people down with words of death? Or will you transform others with words of life?

TOTALLY

TRANSFORMED

FUN

8 The blessing of alcohol

Have you noticed how many ready-made excuses are used in this world? It seems as if people can break any commitment they like, as long as they have a plausible excuse:

"Sorry, I can't make it. I've got a family thing."

"Sorry to let you down—work has called me in."

Nothing wrong if these excuses are **true,** but so many times, we probably suspect that these excuses are just a cover-up for STABO situations (Subject To A Better Offer). That is, you told your friend that you would come around to their place, but while you were on the way, you got a text message from a bunch of other friends inviting you to a night on the town, so you decided to ditch your first commitment. You can't say that to your original friend, can you? So you make up an excuse. (*Shame on you!!*)

Of course, the time you see the most excuses being trotted out is when a guy and a girl are breaking up, when the **breaker** says to the **breakee** things like…

"It's not you, it's me." (Translation: "It's you!")

"I need to find myself." (Translation: "I need to lose you.")

"Let's just be friends." (Translation: "If we run into each other again, please don't make a scene!")

I don't mind following Jesus,
but I want to have fun first.

Hmm. They sound like flimsy excuses to me!

So what do you reckon is the world's biggest excuse for not becoming a Christian? Of all the reasons that are ever given for someone not bothering to follow Jesus, what is the Number 1 popular excuse? I've been working with teenagers for over 30 years, and I can tell you that over the decades the reason hasn't changed.

When I talk with teenagers and I ask them: "Why don't you want to be a Christian?", here is the Number 1 all-time most popular answer:

"I want to have fun."

It comes in many forms, but it's the same excuse.

> *"I don't mind following Jesus, but I want to have fun first."*

> *"If I become a Christian, I've got to do all those boring Christian things."*

> *"All the naughty things are the fun things."*

> *"If I disobey God, I will enjoy life more than if I obey him."*

66

THE MISSION TO HAVE FUN

That's the most popular excuse that non-Christians give. Let me tell you the sad thing. Deep down many Christians believe it too!

Yep, I know you're probably a Christian. I know you're following Jesus.
I know you're wanting to honour God. But come on, be honest. Deep down you believe that if you REALLY want to have fun, you have to disobey God to do it. Because if you didn't believe that, you wouldn't sin. The reason we sin is that we think it will be more fun than not sinning. Deep down most of us really think like that.

Being a young person in the 21st century means you're on a mission. The mission of our age seems to be—to do anything you can to have a good time. If we look at your age group, they are hard at work—week in week out— **making sure they have a good time.**

You want to have fun, don't you? You want to enjoy yourself? You don't want to end up with a life that is dull, colourless and boring? So you keep looking—desperately—for things that will give you a good time. You still keep thinking that there are things you can have that will really make you happy. Even stuff which your brain tells you will destroy you, you still believe it will make you happy.

Things like alcohol. Drugs. Sex. Going out and getting smashed. I have lots of young friends who are **Facebook Friends** and so many times their "Status Update" reads: **"Got hammered last night. Wild night on the town."** Some have even gained notoriety by inviting everyone to trash their parents' house by posting their party on the internet!

IF YOU REALLY BELIEVE

If you really believe that you will have more fun if you disobey God, what are you actually saying about your relationship with God?

"Jesus—I don't trust you to give me the best life possible."

Are you really saying that? Do you honestly believe that if you follow what Jesus says, you'll miss out on things in life that will be good for you?

Remember what Jesus said…

John 10:10
I have come that you may have life, and have it to the full.

Are you actually saying: **"Jesus—you're lying. You don't give life to the full. I'll have more fun if I sin."?**

If you want to follow Jesus, God is not calling you to live a second-rate life. Don't get the idea that living as a Christian means you stop having fun. That over on one side are all the non-Christians—and they're doing all the fun things. And over on the other side are all the Christians— and they're living a life which is dull, colourless and boring.

Come on—do you ever think that? You know that following Jesus is right—you know that eventually when you die you will be rewarded in heaven forever—but you think that living as a Christian NOW means you sort of miss out on all the good stuff.

God is not like that. God is not a mean and stingy God who wants to take away all the good things that you could have. God does not look down and think: **"Hold the phone—they're enjoying themselves—stop it—stop it—stop it!"** God doesn't look down—and as soon as he sees us enjoying ourselves he makes up a commandment to tell us that we shouldn't!

God is just not like that. The Bible clearly shows us that God wants the best for you. God wants you to experience everything that is good for you. If you trust God, you will live the best life of anyone. God is a God who loves to satisfy his people.

Do you really trust that God wants the best for you? Here's what you've have to believe. That if there's something that is going to be good for you—God says **"Do it"**. And he only says **"Don't do it"** if he knows it will be bad for you.

Do you actually believe that? Do you actually think that one of God's main jobs is to stop you having fun? Right now I want to talk with you about the one topic that is most associated with parties and fun. In most circles it's the essential element for having fun. Most people believe **"You can't have a party without it".** Most people believe **"You can't have fun without it".**

And yet this one element causes more pain and destruction in the world than anything else. In most official reports, it's been described as "The world's biggest drug problem". 1 word. 7 letters.

ALCOHOL

Before we get carried away, let me tell you what God thinks about alcohol. Let's get a summary sentence about what the Bible says about alcohol.

ALCOHOL IS GOOD!

Alcohol is good. Alcohol is a good gift from God. Alcohol has been given to us by God for our enjoyment.

Does that surprise you? Check this out with me:

a) It's a gift from God

Psalms 104:13-15

God waters the mountains from his upper chambers; the earth is satisfied by the fruit of his work. He makes grass grow for the cattle, he makes plants for man to cultivate—he brings forth food from the earth: he makes wine that gladdens the heart of man…

Plain and simple. Alcohol is a gift from God for you to enjoy. Serious? Serious!

b) It's a *reward* from God

Proverbs 3:9-10

Honour the LORD with your wealth, with the first fruits of all your crops; then your barns will be filled to overflowing, and your vats will brim over with new wine.

God says to his Old Testament people:

"If you are generous with your money—and give freely to my work, then I will bless you with lots of food and lots of wine."

69

Do you actually think that one of God's main jobs is to stop you having fun?

God uses the picture of "great food and great alcohol" to symbolise the rewards that he gives his faithful people. Isn't it interesting? When God was thinking of ways to describe the wonderful reward he would have for his faithful people, one of the descriptions he thought of was that we would have *lots of wine.*

c) It's a symbol of God's new creation

Have you ever wondered what will it be like to live with God forever? When God is describing what his new creation will be like, he uses pictures to symbolise how great eternity will be.

> **Joel 3:17-18**
>
> *Then you will know that I, the LORD your God, dwell in Zion, my holy hill. Jerusalem will be holy; never again will foreigners invade her. In that day the mountains will drip new wine, and the hills will flow with milk; all the ravines of Judah will run with water.*

Interesting! When God wants to describe what his new, perfect world will be like—where we can enjoy him forever—he includes the picture of a mountain that will **drip new wine!**

d) Jesus drank alcohol

John the Baptist (Jesus' cousin—who lived around the same time as Jesus) made a special vow to God that he would restrict himself to certain foods, and that he would not drink alcohol. Many people did this. But some people criticised John for his strict practices. When Jesus came, he took the more normal approach—he ate most regular food—he drank most regular wine. And guess what? People criticised him as well!

> **Luke 7:33-34**
>
> *For John the Baptist came neither eating bread nor drinking*

*wine, and you say, 'He has a demon.' The Son of Man [Jesus]
came eating and drinking, and you say, 'Here is a glutton and a
drunkard, a friend of tax collectors and 'sinners'.*

Alcohol is not a bad thing. Jesus drank it.

e) Jesus manufactured and supplied alcohol

Do you remember Jesus' first miracle? He was at the wedding of a friend in
Cana, and eventually the wine ran out. What did Jesus do? Did he say:
**"Well, let this be a lesson to you. Wine is bad. And now it's all run
out, how about we all have a nice cup of iced tea"?** No. He got some
water pots, and turned the water into wine so that everyone would have
plenty to drink. And yes, I have heard some of my dear Christian friends say:
"It must have been non-alcoholic wine" —but that's not the assessment
of the people at the wedding who actually drank it.

They said:

> ### John 2:10
> *"Everyone brings out the choice wine first and then the cheaper
> wine after the guests have had too much to drink; but you have
> saved the best till now.*

Pretty impressive report! The wine that Jesus made was **better** than
anything else they had ever tasted.

Can we summarise where we have got to so far?

- Alcohol is not a bad thing.
- It is a good gift from God.
- Jesus himself drank wine.
- Jesus' first miracle was to turn
  water into wine.
- He manufactured alcohol and
  supplied it to others.

> Alcohol is not a bad thing.
> Jesus drank it.

Now just before you all race out to the nearest pub and get yourself
absolutely sozzled… just before you stop hanging out at the local fast food
joint and start hanging out at the local boozer… **please read the next
chapter!** You need to know there are extreme dangers with alcohol!

The danger of alcohol

THE PHYSICAL PROBLEM

You don't have to look far to see the enormous problem that the abuse of alcohol causes in our community. Here are some statistics from my country:

- Alcohol is the second largest cause of drug-related deaths and hospitalisations (after tobacco).
- Alcohol is the main cause of deaths on roads. Recently over 2,000 deaths of the total 7,000 deaths of people under 65 years were related to alcohol.

If you've ever been in a situation where a whole lot of people have got out of control because they were fuelled up with booze—you know it's an ugly scene. If you've ever seen someone else slowly drinking themselves into a state of being blind drunk, you know it's not a pretty sight.

You don't have to go far to see the mess that people make with their lives with alcohol.

My son Josh, as a young adult, went on a tour of Europe. Each night they were put into twin-share accommodation in whatever hotel they were staying in. One night, his room-mate came in very late—long after Josh was in bed. His room-mate had indulged in a vast over-consumption of alcohol.

Josh was woken when he discovered that his drunken room-mate was peeing all over him!

My own dad—who died when I was 11—would often come home very drunk. He ploughed so much of his money into his drinking habit that he did not just come home out of control and angry, he also came home penniless.

The Bible understands the mess we can get into with excessive alcohol.

> **Proverbs 23:29-35**
> "Who has woe? Who has sorrow? Who has strife? Who has complaints? Who has needless bruises? Who has bloodshot eyes? Those who linger over wine, who go to sample bowls of mixed wine. Do not gaze at wine when it is red, when it sparkles in the cup, when it goes down smoothly! In the end it bites like a snake and poisons like a viper. Your eyes will see strange sights and your mind imagine confusing things. You will be like one sleeping on the high seas, lying on top of the rigging. "They hit me," you will say, "but I'm not hurt! They beat me, but I don't feel it! When will I wake up so I can find another drink?"

It will come as no surprise to find out that the Bible absolutely prohibits drunkenness among God's people. It won't shock you in the least to discover that God says to you: **"Drunkenness is out!"** But the reasons that God gives in his warnings about drunkenness—his reasons might surprise you.

THE CONTROL PROBLEM

> **Ephesians 5:18 (paraphrase)**
> Don't be drunk with wine, because that will ruin your life. Instead, let the Holy Spirit fill and control you.

You cannot get a clearer verse which shows you that getting drunk is absolutely wrong for a Christian. It is never to be tolerated among God's people.

"Don't be drunk with wine."
"Don't get drunk."

If you think that drinking too much is an okay thing a for a Christian to do, then you need to look at God's clear command: "Do not get drunk". You need to obey God's clear command: "Do not get drunk".

But look at the reasons that God gives you for not getting drunk! There are two reasons here. See if you can spot them.

Ephesians 5:18

Don't be drunk with wine, because that will ruin your life.
Instead, let the Holy Spirit fill and control you. (NLT)

Reason 1: It will ruin your life.

Reason 2: Rather than getting drunk, what is the alternative that is recommended?

Ephesians 5:18

Don't be drunk with wine, because that will ruin your life.
Instead…

Now if you were writing the Bible, how would you finish that sentence?

Ephesians 5:18

Don't be drunk with wine, because that will ruin your life.
Instead…

...don't drink?

...drink in moderation?

...drink lots of water?

...drink lots of Coke?

...drink lots of hot chocolate?

Ephesians 5:18
*Don't be drunk with wine, because that will ruin your life.
Instead,* **let the Holy Spirit fill and control you.**

How is letting the Holy Spirit fill you an alternative to getting drunk? What does it mean to be filled with the Holy Spirit?

a) A continuous event

Being filled with God's Spirit is not meant to be a one-off event.

"20 years ago I got filled with God's Spirit and I'm glad I never have to go through that again!"

No—the word for **filled** means **go on being filled.** The sense of the word is that you should **continually** be filled with the Holy Spirit.

Why do you need to be continually filled with the Holy Spirit? It doesn't mean: **"You didn't get enough of the Spirit when you became a Christian—and we need to top you up".** And it doesn't mean: **"We need to fill you up with the Spirit, coz you've let some of the Spirit leak out of you".**

b) A question of control

It's a question of what controls you. Being **filled** with the Spirit really

Think you can handle it?

76

Don't let alcohol control you.
Let God control you.

means being **controlled** by the Spirit. It's like saying about someone: **"He was filled with anger."** What that really means is—he was **controlled** by anger.

Ephesians 5:18 is saying **"Don't let alcohol control you. Let God control you."** The reason that you are to avoid drunkenness at any cost is that it is a barrier to God working in your life. Because when you're under the influence of booze, then you're not under the influence of God's Holy Spirit.

- When you're affected by too much alcohol, then you won't hear God speak clearly.

- When you're affected by too much alcohol, then you won't obey God clearly.

- When you're affected by too much alcohol, then you won't be able to teach others about God clearly.

THE LEADERSHIP PROBLEM

That's why drunkenness is specifically listed as totally unacceptable for a Christian leader. Imagine if you were meant to be ministering to others, but you were too affected by alcohol to be of help to anyone?

It actually happened in the Old Testament. The priests—who were the spiritual leaders of God's people—were getting drunk. They weren't able to do the ministry that God wanted!

Isaiah 28:7-8
And these also stagger from wine and reel from beer: Priests and prophets stagger from beer and are befuddled with wine; they reel from beer, they stagger when seeing visions, they stumble when rendering decisions. All the tables are covered with vomit and there is not a spot without filth.

THE DRUNKENNESS PROBLEM

If you fully understand that the biblical reason why you don't get drunk has to do with what is **controlling** you, then we might have to redefine what we mean by the term **"getting drunk".**

Most people will admit that falling down face first in your own vomit—yeah—that's drunk. But what about getting a bit tipsy… getting a bit funny… becoming the life of the party—is that okay?

If the biblical reason to stay right away from drunkenness has to do with what is controlling you, what is influencing you… then anytime that alcohol is starting to have an influence on you—I think that's drunk. Anytime your personality is starting to change because you're drinking—I think that's drunk. Anytime there's any change in you because of your drinking—that's influence, that's control, that's drunk.

> *"Anytime there's any change in you because of your drinking—that's in-fluence—that's control—that's being drunk."*

You can drink a certain small amount—and it might have no effect on you. You then drink one more drink over that limit—and you start to be affected by it. I think that's drunk. Here's the problem: the only way to find out your limit is to actually go over it! Do you see the problem?

I got drunk once. I'm not very proud of it at all. It was before I became a Christian—but that is no excuse. It was the end of my final year at school. It

I lost control...

was the last day at school and one of my class-mates had an unofficial **after-party** at his place. The whole of my school year attended. There was a keg at this after-party. All the beer you could want. Freely available on tap. I drank too much. I lost control. I fell over. I spewed.

I guess I can understand why people might try getting drunk once. But I can't for the life of me understand why anyone would try it twice!

The Bible's problem with drunkenness has to do with—"What is influencing and controlling your life?" Is it alcohol—or is it God?

10 So—have you thought about…?

Of course, there are other issues in the Bible that also govern how much alcohol we will drink, or whether we drink at all.

THE LAW

Laws vary from country to country, but generally every country has some laws to protect young, growing bodies from the effect of alcohol. In my part of the planet, there are lots of laws prohibiting the sale, distribution and consumption of alcohol to Under-18's. There are good reasons for those laws. Alcohol can do so much damage to young growing bodies. Alcohol can do so much damage to growing brains. So most communities have passed some sort of laws that restrict supplying alcohol to younger people.

So if you're a Christian—and something is against the law—then you are defying God if you break the law. The Bible makes this clear:

> ### Romans 13:1-2
> *Everyone must submit himself to the governing authorities, for there is no authority except that which God has established. The authorities that exist have been established by God. Consequently, he who rebels against the authority is rebelling against what God has instituted, and those who do so will bring judgment on themselves.*

I think God's attitude is this: **if something's illegal—then don't do it.** And while drugs are not specifically mentioned in the Bible, all the information about the abuse of alcohol also applies to them. But it's clearer cut with drugs: if drugs are illegal—then that's reason enough for a Christian to have nothing to do with them.

If you are living at home with your parents, they have the right to tell you how to behave!

YOUR PARENTS

Christian children are called on to obey their parents. If you are living at home under their authority, then it is reasonable that they can lay down guidelines for how you are to behave. We'll look at that more in later chapters.

But here's the bottom line: if you're living at home under the authority of your parents—and your parents have told you not to drink alcohol—then you would be defying God to disobey them.

And defying God is not a good idea!

YOUR HEALTH

1 Corinthians 6:19-20
Do you not know that your body is a temple of the Holy Spirit, who is in you, whom you have received from God? You are not your own; you were bought at a price. Therefore honour God with your body.

Christians are called on to honour God with their bodies. They are described as being a temple of the Holy Spirit. Your body is where God chooses to live. So we honour it. We are called on to look after it. To keep it healthy. Not to trash it.

Sure—a little alcohol might be medicinally helpful for an adult. And remember that alcohol is a wonderful gift from our loving heavenly Father. But there is overwhelming evidence that excessive alcohol consumption—

especially in young and growing bodies—is terribly bad for you. If drinking too much alcohol is trashing your body—then that is another good enough reason for a Christian not to do it.

YOUR MONEY

God calls on you to use your money wisely for his glory. Alcohol is expensive.

If you end up spending lots and lots of money on alcohol, then that might not be honouring God with your money. Enough said?

WEAKER CHRISTIANS

1 Corinthians 8:13
Therefore, if what I eat causes my brother to fall into sin, I will never eat meat again, so that I will not cause him to fall.

Paul was dealing with a different issue in this passage. For the Christians in Corinth, back in those days, the meat at their local butcher shop had been offered up to a false God. Here's the question they were asking Paul's help on: **"Is it okay for a Christian to eat meat that has been offered up to an idol?"** The answer is: *"Yes—no problems—it's just meat"*. But what if a weaker Christian—who doesn't understand that it's *"just meat"*—sees you doing it, and thinks it's okay to worship a false god?

There's a lot at steak...

Here is God's answer:

1 Corinthians 8:13
Therefore, if what I eat causes my brother to fall into sin, I will never eat meat again, so that I will not cause him to fall.

That's why many Christian leaders don't touch alcohol at all. Not because there's anything wrong with it. There's nothing in the Bible says I can't go down to the pub after the church youth group and have a quiet beer. But here's my problem; even though I am within my rights to have a quiet drink as a Christian, then I don't want a weaker Christian to look at me— see that I go off and have my drink—and somehow misinterpret that to mean I have given them the green light to drink as much as they like!

With great freedom comes great responsibility...

That's an extra thing I do as a youth leader. The leaders at our church don't **have** to do that. And I want to honour leaders who drink alcohol in accordance with what God says. They have perfect freedom in Christ to do just that. But how your action will affect a weaker Christian is yet another issue you need to think through when you're old enough to drink alcohol.

BECOMING A PROBLEM DRINKER

Often you can have a real alcohol problem without realising it. Usually everybody else realises it before you do! There are many groups set up specifically to help people who are affected by alcoholism. If you drink at all—you might like to take this test designed by Alcoholics Anonymous to help people work out whether they have any serious issues with alcohol:

Alcoholics Anonymous suggests that if you could honestly answer "yes" to four or more questions, then you might well have a problem with alcohol. This doesn't mean you're a bad person—it simply means that you need some help to deal with this issue.

Of course, one way to make sure that you never end up with any of these problems—don't start drinking!

1. Have you ever decided to stop drinking for a week or so, but only lasted for a couple of days?   ☐ yes ☐ no

2. Do you wish people would mind their own business about your drinking—stop telling you what to do?   ☐ yes ☐ no

3. Have you ever switched from one kind of drink to another in the hope that this would keep you from getting drunk?   ☐ yes ☐ no

4. Have you had to have an eye-opener upon awakening during the past year? Do you need a drink to get started, or to stop shaking?   ☐ yes ☐ no

5. Do you envy people who can drink without getting into trouble?   ☐ yes ☐ no

6. Have you had problems connected with drinking during the past year?   ☐ yes ☐ no

7. Has your drinking caused trouble at home?   ☐ yes ☐ no

8. Do you ever try to get "extra" drinks at a party because you do not get enough?   ☐ yes ☐ no

9. Do you tell yourself you can stop drinking any time you want to, even though you keep getting drunk when you don't mean to?   ☐ yes ☐ no

10. Have you missed days of work or school because of drinking?   ☐ yes ☐ no

11. Do you have "blackouts"? A "blackout" is when you have been drinking hours or days which we cannot remember.   ☐ yes ☐ no

12. Have you ever felt that your life would be better if you did not drink?   ☐ yes ☐ no

If you answered "Yes" to four or more of these questions, talk to someone about it immediately…

Do you trust God to give you the best life ever?

THE BOTTOM LINE

Let's put together everything we've learned:

1. **Alcohol is good. It is a great gift from God.**

2. **Abusing alcohol is disobedient to God. There is no place for a Christian who keeps getting drunk.**

Hey—if you've been drunk once or twice, and you've confessed that to God, he's forgiven you—you can be absolutely sure of that. But if you **keep on** getting drunk—that is a sure sign that you need the help of your brothers and sisters so that you can start to take obeying God seriously. If you honestly think that you can't deal with this alone, then go to a trusted Christian friend, so that together you might deal with this under God's mighty hand.

Here's the key issue: Do you trust God enough that—if you obey him—he will give you the best life ever? Or do you think that to really have fun you have to disobey him?

Do you want to have fun? Do you want to love life? Do you want to see good days? Then God tells you how to do it. Don't forget that he has already given you everything you need to be totally transformed. Do you trust him enough to actually do what he says?

1 Peter 3:10-12

Whoever would love life and see good days must keep his tongue from evil and his lips from deceitful speech. He must turn from evil and do good; he must seek peace and pursue it. For the eyes of the Lord are on the righteous and his ears are attentive to their prayer, but the face of the Lord is against those who do evil.

- Do you really want to have fun?
- Do you think you've got to get drunk to have the most fun?
- Do you honestly trust God to give you the most fun possible?

TOTALLY TRANSFORMED SUBMISSION

I STILL LIVE WITH MY PARENTS

11 The joy of submitting

Have you ever noticed that guys and girls are very different in the spontaneous games they play? If there's a bunch of girls or guys standing around and they **spontaneously** *start playing a game, I've noticed there is often a remarkable difference between the games they play.*

Many girls seem to automatically play **co-operative** games. I've seen younger ones suddenly produce ropes and all join in a skipping game to the tune of *"Teddy Bear, Teddy Bear, turn around..."*. I've seen other girls start playing these amazing games with wool wrapped around their hands and fingers, where they produce the most spectacular geometric patterns. And then there are the clapping games! They stand in a circle and produce the most tightly choreographed clapping routine, which is simply a wonder to behold!

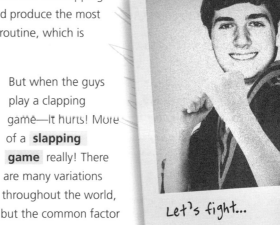

Let's fight...

But when the guys play a clapping game—It hurts! More of a **slapping game** really! There are many variations throughout the world, but the common factor in all guys' slapping games is **pain!** Some

Let's play...

91

of their other games are equally competitive. The very names of these games give away their fierce competitive (and painful) nature of these spontaneous games—

Punch for punch—Bleeding knuckles—Chicken scratch—Mercy.

But, I suspect that the all-time favourite spontaneous game when there's a couple of guys standing around is **wrestling!** There will be two guys—who are the best of friends—and one moment they're laughing and talking with each other, high-fiving and slapping each other on the back—and the next minute they are physically going for each other like mortal enemies! They are rolling on the ground—putting each other in headlocks—twisting each other's limbs to cause exquisite pain—and the whole rumble continues until the guy on top eventually asks "Give in?"—and the guy on the bottom reluctantly submits.

When we think about **submission,** that's the picture that most of us have. You submit because you're forced to. And if you don't submit—you know there's more pain coming! Most of us hate submitting because we **have** to!

So, you're at school, or on a camp, and you're waiting in line for your food. And some guy pushes in right in front of you.

"Hey—quit pushing in!"

"What are you going to do about it"

You decide to let him in and avoid a stand-up fight. **That's submission.**

You submit because you're forced to. And most of us hate submitting because we have to. As soon as anyone raises the issue of submission, most of us are thinking: ***"I don't want to submit like that. I don't want to be forced to give in".***

I understand that. I hate being forced to give in when I don't want to. But can I introduce you to a completely different concept?

JOYFUL SUBMISSION

Joyful submission? Yep! Joyful submission means you will voluntarily and joyfully submit to someone if the benefits outweigh the disadvantages.

92

Your mum says: ***"I want you to clean all the toilets at home every week … and I'll give you \$1000 per week to do it!"*** Most of us could submit to that.

There's a girl or guy whom you want to ask out—but you haven't got the guts—but one day they come up to you and say: ***"Hey—can we go and see a movie together?"*** You could probably submit to that!

You want to be an awesome football player—and one of the top professional football payers in the world, the one you idolise the most, he watches you play a game and says to you: ***"I hear you want to be an awesome football player. I see potential in you. Here's the deal: free of charge, I will be your personal coach. I will work you very hard, but if you stick with me I will take you all the way to the top. Deal?"*** I suspect you could probably submit to that!

There will come a day where everyone in the world will have to submit to Jesus whether they want to or not.

You will voluntarily and joyfully submit to someone if the benefits outweigh the disadvantages. That's what happens when you become a Christian!

You make a decision that any negatives in following Jesus are clearly outweighed by the benefits. Sure, there are some hard steps in handing

We submit because Jesus did..

your life over to Christ… but eventually you work out that the benefits of being made **totally transformed** far outweigh the difficult stuff.

If Jesus has called you to follow him—he has called you to live a life of submission. I want to show you from the Bible how joyful submission can be one of the biggest buzzes in your life.

SUBMITTING TO GOD

1. God demands submission

Isaiah 45:22-23

Turn to me and be saved, all you ends of the earth; for I am God, and there is no other. By myself I have sworn, my mouth has uttered in all integrity a word that will not be revoked: Before me every knee will bow; by me every tongue will swear.

God says that one day everyone will bow down before him. There will come a day when everyone in the world will have to submit to Jesus whether they want to or not. Sometimes you might **think** that you're more powerful than God, but believe me, if it comes to a showdown between God and you, God will win every time.

2. Jesus submits to his Father

The ultimate picture of submission is the way Jesus submits to his Father. The night before he was put to death, Jesus and his disciples were in a garden together, and he told them:

Matthew 26:38

My soul is overwhelmed with sorrow to the point of death.

What an incredibly difficult time that must have been! Jesus was looking forward a few hours to the enormous and agonising task of dying on the cross, and says he is so overwhelmed, he is on the point of death. Clearly, his human will did not want to do it.

So he left the disciples and prayed on his own. He fell onto the ground, face down, and said:

> **Matthew 26:39**
> *My Father, if it is possible, may this cup be taken from me. Yet not as I will, but as you will.*

He asked if there was any way that this cup could be taken away from him. Everything in him was screaming to get away— **but he chose to submit!** He would submit his will to that of the Father, even though it would cost him his life.

You don't just care for yourself... You care about the whole body.

Submission means this: you choose the will of the other person rather than your own. Jesus is the most magnificent example of this.

But God is not the only person whom we are called to submit to!

SUBMITTING TO EACH OTHER

There is an over-riding principle for every Christian in Ephesians:

> **Ephesians 5:21**
> *Submit to one another out of reverence for Christ*

Christians are called to **submit to each other** so that Christ is honoured.

"Let's stand and sing praise to God!"

Submitting to others means you don't just charge ahead with your own ideas—you listen to other people's thoughts, even when they disagree with you. Submitting to others means that you don't just focus on your own needs. When you become aware of other people's needs, you might leave your own needs aside for a while so that you can love and care for the other person. You don't just care for yourself; you care about the whole body. That's what submitting to each other means.

For example, imagine you are in your church, or your youth group. It's time to sing praise to God. The person who's leading stands at the front—with the whole band behind them—and says to the congregation: **"Let's stand and sing praise to God!"**

Now right at that moment, you might be thinking: **"Yes—I really want to stand and sing"** or you might be thinking: **"My feet are sore—I don't want to stand up—and this isn't my favourite song anyway."** But whatever you are thinking, **you submit to the ministry of your leader by standing up and joining in!**

Imagine what would happen if none of us had the spirit of submission! There'd be some people scattered around the congregation who were dutifully standing and singing; there'd be another bunch sitting down playing cards; there'd be a few more who tuned into their ipods; some of the girls might start skipping games and some of the guys would be wrestling in the corner— **it would be chaos!** (My apologies if I have just described what your youth group looks like!) But if you all join in, that's what submitting to other Christians looks like— Christ is honoured and everybody grows.

That's the way your own body works. Your legs say: ***"I want to play football"*** but your bladder says: ***"I really have to empty"***. What will you do? Most likely your legs will submit to your bladder—not

We are called to submit to God

just for the sake of the bladder—but for the benefit of the whole body! (And of course the legs will also be better off in the long run—if you get what I mean…)

A Christian group should not be one where everyone is trying to have their own way. Where everyone is trying to outdo everyone else so they can be the funniest… the loudest… the smelliest… A Christian group should be one where the various members are ready to submit to each other.

Does that describe your youth group? Does that describe your Bible-study group? Where you all joyfully submit to each other? Or does your group look more as if everyone is fighting to be the centre of attention?

So, we are called to submit to God; we are called to submit to each other. There is also another group of people whom we are particularly called to submit to:

1. Community leaders

Romans 13:1-2

Everyone must submit himself to the governing authorities, for there is no authority except that which God has established.

The authorities that exist have been established by God. Consequently, he who rebels against the authority is rebelling against what God has instituted, and those who do so will bring judgment on themselves.

Take me to your leader...

Look carefully at what God is saying in the above verses. These verses are mainly talking about our community leaders. Our government… our judicial system… our police force… those who have been placed in authority over our community. Read it through, and you can see that God is saying…

- **You must submit to those in authority.**
- **The authorities that exist have been placed there by God.**
- **If you rebel against these authorities, you are rebelling against God.**

It's not saying that everyone in authority is perfect. It's not saying you will always agree with them. It's not even saying they will always act in your best interest. In fact, sometimes you will be hard done by! Remember, Paul wrote these words while the Roman Government ruled over God's people with a cruel fist of iron!

Look again at what God teaches us about submission in these verses:

- **You must submit to those in authority.**
- **The authorities that exist have been placed there by God.**
- **If you rebel against these authorities, you are rebelling against God.**

So if I break the speed limit, I'm not just running the risk of being caught, I am in fact being disobedient to God. If I am illegally downloading music or copying software, I'm actually being disobedient to God.

Do you see the implications of this? That means I should not slow down to the speed limit because I know there is a speed camera ahead—I should slow down to the speed limit to honour Jesus— *whether there's a speed camera there or not!*

Wow! Did you ever imagine that submission was such a big issue?

That doesn't mean you have to **agree** with the law. That doesn't mean that you have to **like** the law. You can even protest as much as you like so that the law gets changed! (And throughout the centuries, Christians have been responsible for protesting against many unjust laws and finally getting them changed!) You can argue against a law as much as you like! (That's why our governments have an **opposition party!**) But it means that while the law exists—unless it is forcing you to disobey God— **you keep it!**

What about other people who have been placed in authority over you? What about if you are a school student and you have teachers and principals placed in authority over you? As a Christian, are you meant to submit to them? In *The Simpsons*, should Bart submit to Principal Skinner? At your school, should you submit to your school principal?

Look back at Romans 13:1-2. The answer is **yes!**

Should I submit to a school teacher? A police officer? My sporting coach? If you are under their authority, the answer is **yes!** Not because you like them or agree with them. You submit to them to honour Christ.

Important note: *If a person in authority is abusing you, or causing you to disobey God, you do not have to keep submitting to them. More about this in the next chapter!*

So the Bible is pretty clear about submitting to community leaders. What about church leaders?

2. Spiritual leaders

Hebrews 13:17

Obey your leaders and submit to their authority. They keep watch over you as men who must give an account. Obey them so that their work will be a joy, not a burden, for that would be of no advantage to you.

This verse is talking about your **spiritual leaders—*"they keep watch over you as men who must give an account".*** The same principle of joyful submission that we are called on to show to God, and to each other, and to our civil leaders, we are also called on to show to our **spiritual leaders.**

Think about the people who are in spiritual authority over you. The senior pastor at your church… your youth pastor… your Bible-study leader… your leader on a camp… how are you going to submit to them? Look carefully at the words near the end of Hebrews 13:17: ***"Obey them so that their work will be a joy, not a burden…"***

Think about those who have spiritual leadership over you. Do you make their job a joy or a burden? Do you go out of your way to make life easy for them, or do you push your resistance so far that you actually make life harder for them? Think about it! If you genuinely work out that you are making life harder for your spiritual leaders, go now and confess this to them—and in repentance determine that you will never be so unsubmissive again!

We now get to the group of people who are the absolute most fun for you to submit to— **next chapter!**

12 Submitting to parents

Okay! This is where the fun starts! Let's see what God says about the way we should treat our parents!

Ephesians 6:1-3
Children, obey your parents in the Lord, for this is right. "Honour your father and mother"—which is the first commandment with a promise—"that it may go well with you and that you may enjoy long life on the earth."

"Children, obey your parents..." —seriously, that's what the Bible says. I know what it's like to be a young person at home. I looked and looked and looked in the Bible to see if I could come up with something different for you, but look at it yourself—that's what God says!

But let's look a bit more closely. I want you to discover the **joy** of submitting to your parents. Here are four reasons why God thinks this is a good idea…

Who? me?

1. "IN THE LORD"

Ephesians 6:1
*Children, obey your parents **in the Lord**…"*

There's the first reason why obeying your parents might be a good idea. You obey them *"in the Lord"*. You obey them as if you're obeying Jesus. That means, if you're rebelling against the authority that God has placed over you, you are rebelling against God.

Isn't God clever to give you such a nifty way to obey him day in day out? When God thought to himself: **"How can I give children endless opportunities each day to honour me?"** he came up with this brilliant idea: **"I know! I'll get them to obey their parents! Every time they obey their parents, they're honouring me!"**

That's right! Every time you obey your parents—you are obeying God! What a blast! That doesn't mean you have to agree with them; it doesn't mean you have to like some of the household rules they come up with; and it doesn't mean you're not allowed to protest from time to time. But in the end, if you want to honour Jesus, you joyfully submit.

So if your dad says: **"You are NOT going to church tonight!"** —what do you do? Here's the question to ask—would Jesus be honoured if you sneaked out and went?

2. "FOR THIS IS RIGHT"

Ephesians 6:1

Children, obey your parents in the Lord, for this is right…

Someone has to be in charge of your family. Someone has to take responsibility. Can you believe that your parents might actually have more experience of life than you? Is it possible that your parents might have more capacity to provide the things a family needs?

You see, not everybody gets to be the captain. Not everyone gets to make the final decision.

For many years I coached a junior football team. Lots of people had lots of ideas as to how I should run the team. Many of the boys had their own ideas, and certainly, many of their parents always had helpful suggestions as to why I should make their son the star player! And I always listened to them. And I always learned from them. But in the end I had to take the responsibility. I had to take leadership. I was the coach.

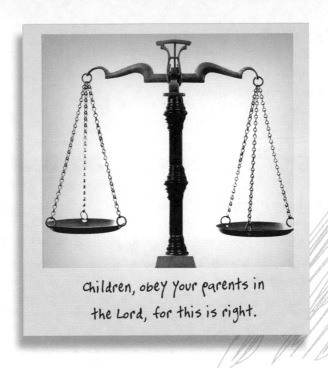

children, obey your parents in
the Lord, for this is right.

Parents have a God-given responsibility to lead their families. And it is right that they should do this. If they abandon that responsibility, they are accountable to God for their failure.

3. IT IS A COMMANDMENT

Ephesians 6:1-2

Children, obey your parents in the Lord, for this is right. "Honour your father and mother"—which is the first commandment with a promise…

If God has made something a commandment, it simply means that he really wants it to happen. That is, God cared enough about that particular issue to include it as a commandment. The commandments show us what is close to God's heart.

If you look through the commandments, you'll see a whole load of stuff that really matters to God. Things like:

- No murder
- No sexual fooling around
- No lying
- No worshipping of false gods
- No stealing

I guess that all makes sense. But in the list of the "Top Ten" things that really matter to God, he includes **"Honour your father and your mother..."** (Exodus 20:12). That is, God makes a very strong statement: **"We can't have kids being disobedient to their parents!"** This is something that he wants everyone to follow. That's why he made it one of the big ten. When you decide to submit to God, you are also saying: "I will submit to this commandment". And remember that they are the ten *commandments*, not the ten *suggestions*!

"Children, obey your parents in the Lord, for this is right. "Honour your father and mother"—which is the first commandment with a promise—"that it may go well with you and that you may enjoy long life on the earth."

Ephesians 6:1-3

Children, obey your parents in the Lord, for this is right. "Honour your father and mother"—which is the first commandment with a promise—"that it may go well with you and that you may enjoy long life on the earth."

Can you believe that when you are joyfully submitting to your parents the same way Jesus did, things will go better at home?

Sure, I know—parents are sometimes stupid. You know more about setting up the Wii, using Facebook, accessing the internet, sending an email or a text—you know more about these things than your parents ever will!

And sometimes they will make really dumb decisions.

But imagine a world where kids were in charge of running families. Do you think family life would be any better? With all their failings, your parents are **probably** the most qualified people in your family to be in charge!

Indeed, when the Bible says that you should submit to your parents — ***"that it may go well with you and that you may enjoy long life on the earth"*** —there was a very good reason as to why this was so! Look at what was meant to happen to disobedient children back in the Old Testament days!

Deuteronomy 21:18-21

If a man has a stubborn and rebellious son who does not obey his father and mother and will not listen to them when they discipline him, his father and mother shall take hold of him and bring him to the elders at the gate of his town. They shall say to the elders, "This son of ours is stubborn and

rebellious. He will not obey us. He is a profligate and a
drunkard." Then all the men of his town shall stone him to death.
You must purge the evil from among you. All Israel will hear of it
and be afraid.

Wow! Can you see how seriously God takes the issue of children who will not obey their parents! God was forming the nation of Israel—he was moulding a people who would belong to him and represent him to every other nation—and he says very clearly: ***"I cannot have disobedient kids in my community."***

13 Three tricky questions

The Bible is pretty clear on what the role of a child is in their family. If you are young—and you live at home under your parents' authority—then the Bible is clear that the godly way for you to respond to them is to joyfully submit to them.

However, here are three tricky questions…

1. IS THERE AN AGE LIMIT ON OBEYING YOUR PARENTS?

This was much simpler in Bible times. You were a child at home up until you were aged around 13 or 14. Then your parents would select a partner for you, you would get married, establish your new family, and promptly have your own kids. There was a fairly clear division between when you were a child at home under your parents' authority, and when you became a parent with responsibilities towards your own children.

I STILL LIVE WITH MY **PARENTS**

34, and still not left home!

These days—things are not that cut and dried. Young people are maturing physically younger and younger, and yet staying at home for longer and longer! It is very common these days to have full-grown adults still living at home with their parents.

So, is there an **age limit** on when you have to still obey your parents? The Bible is not crystal clear on this, but let's check out a few key issues.

The Bible calls on us to **honour** our parents [1]. This is a lifetime commitment. There is no age limit on this. All Christians are called on to honour their

---

1 Exodus 20:12, Deuteronomy 5:16, Matthew 15:4, Matthew 19:19, Mark 7:10, Mark 10:19, Luke 18:20, Ephesians 6:2.

I'm not ignoring you — I'm just listening to my fingers...

parents throughout their lifetime. My own mum is now in her eighties, and I still strive to honour her in any way I can.

The Bible also calls us to **obey** our parents.[2] So… what's the dividing line between honouring our parents and obeying our parents? Is there an age limit on when you no longer need to obey them? There are no clear directions on this in the Bible, but here is my best shot: you are certainly called on to **obey** your parents while you are **under-age** (that is, while your parents are still legally responsible for you). I also believe that once you become an adult in your own right **and you choose to live at home under your parents' authority,** then you are still called on to **obey** them.

Of course, the wise parent will be very careful as to how much they demand of their adult children's obedience! But I think if you choose to keep living at your parents' home while you are an adult, then it's reasonable that you conform to the **house rules.** And if you are a young adult, still living at home, and you're finding your parents' house rules **unbearable,** then I have a suggestion— ***move out!***

Does it make sense, once you have become an adult yourself, and you have moved out of home, that while you will always **honour** your parents, there is no call on you to keep **obeying** them? I haven't lived at home with my mum since I was married over thirty years ago. Tonight, if I wanted to stay out late at night, I wouldn't ring my mum and ask permission first!

---

2 Ephesians 6:1, Colossians 3:20.

2. WHAT IF MY PARENTS ARE ABUSING ME?

Sometimes things go wrong in families. Sometimes even parents—the very people who are meant to love you—can end up abusing their children. Abusing them physically, sexually or emotionally. Let's be clear: **no form of abuse can be tolerated in any community.** There are straightforward guidelines in most countries that require any forms of child abuse to be reported to the police so that innocent children can be protected. If you—or anyone you know—is being abused by their parents—or by any adult— **you must let someone know.** If you belong to a church, that's a great place to talk over all sorts of issues and to be supported by people who care about you.

While the Bible is clear that children are to submit to their parents, I'm sure that God would never want you to keep submitting to an abusive parent. You might still **honour** them, but you don't have to **submit** to them. Because by **submitting** to them, you are allowing them to keep sinning. And God would never want you to do anything that encourages anyone else to keep sinning.

If there's any form of abuse in your family— *talk to someone today!* There is a way forward—you don't have to keep facing this by yourself.

This is a much easier question to answer—because there is a clear word from God in the Bible.

Shortly after Jesus ascended back to heaven, Peter and the other apostles were busy telling everyone about Jesus and helping them to believe in him. The authorities were getting very upset with them, and so they threw Peter and the apostles into jail. But God sent an angel to let them out of jail—and the next morning there they were in the temple courts—preaching about Jesus—doing the very thing that the authorities had told them **not** to do.

One of the leaders in authority confronts the apostles:

> **Acts 5:28**
>
> "We gave you strict orders not to teach in this name," he said.
>
> "Yet you have filled Jerusalem with your teaching and are determined to make us guilty of this man's blood."

The apostles' reply?

> **Acts 5:29**
>
> "We must obey God rather than men!"

There you have it! If obeying your parents means you would be disobeying God, then you must obey God before you obey humans. So if your parents say to you: *"I want you to some with us and help us rob a bank",* I think you have every right to say to your parents: *"I honour you and I respect you, but I cannot disobey God like that!"*

What if your dad says: *"I forbid you to attend that church anymore"* —what do you do? Now this is a different case! Don't just confront your dad and declare: *"I don't care what you say. I would be disobeying God by not attending that church. Therefore I choose to obey God rather than you!"* Let's be careful! The Bible certainly tells you not to give up meeting with other Christians,[3] but does it tell you that you must attend this particular church on this particular day? No! The Christ-like response to this command from your dad might be to raise the flag of protest—but in the

_____

3 Hebrews 10:25

end, you honour him, you honour God and you submit. There will be other opportunities to meet with Christians (maybe at school!).

I remember one young guy in our youth group. He was around 14. He had come to Christ, but his family had remained firmly non-Christian. His parents prohibited him from reading his Bible at home. Being a slightly rebellious kid, he continued to read his Bible at home. When his parents discovered his disobedience, they punished him by confining him to his room. I asked him once: *"So what do you do when you're confined to your room?"* He grinned as he gave his answer. *"I read my Bible!"*

You know, to this day, I can never work out whether he did the right thing or not. What do you think?

THE BOTTOM LINE

"I don't want to hear this."

By now you might well be thinking *"I don't want to hear this! I paid good money for this book, and this is not the message I wanted to read! Tell me something I want to hear!"*

I didn't write these words because I thought they were something you **wanted** to hear. I wrote this because it is something you **need** to hear. Where is it hard to live as a totally transformed person? One of the hardest places can be—with your parents at home!

You might have the world's greatest parents. You might have the world's worst parents. You might have non-Christian parents who don't care that much. Or you might have the most oppressive form of parents—Christian parents who care **too much.** You might have remote-control parents—

who are too interested in their own issues to pay any attention to stuff you're doing. Or you could have **helicopter parents** —who always hover around you—never letting you out of their sight—always controlling everything to make sure that you never make a mistake.

The effect on Christian parents

But if you took this submission seriously… if at home you were a model of joyful submission… what effect might it have on your **Christian** parents?

Let me tell you the most probable result. They will most likely see you as more mature. They may well allow you to have more responsibility. And you could be a huge encouragement to them. In fact, you might even challenge them to a higher standard in their own walk with Jesus!

At our church, we've had many parents who have seen the high level of their teenager's discipleship—and have been challenged. They realised that their kids were stronger Christians than they were! Imagine how you would bless your Christian parents if you determined that you would joyfully submit to them!

The effect on non-Christian parents

If you took this seriously … if at home you were a model of joyful submission… what effect might it have on your **non-Christian** parents?

It might just be that they will see the power of Jesus for the first time. It

They are watching you...

might not matter to them that God has the power to create the world. It may mean nothing to them that Jesus has the power to rise from the dead. But when they see that Jesus has the power to change their kid's life—wow! They may start to think: "If Jesus can change the life of my child—well, maybe he might even be able to change my life!"

That's how my mum became a Christian. I was in my late teens when I gave my life to Christ. I was a very young Christian, not a particularly strong Christian, and probably not a very faithful Christian. But my mum saw in me something that she didn't have. And she knew it

was something that she wanted. Over time she came to Christ herself and continues to grow as God's daughter. But it all started from the very tenuous changes that happened in my life when I became a Christian.

A joy, not a burden

Hebrews 13:17

"Obey your leaders and submit to their authority. They keep watch over you as men who must give an account. Obey them so that their work will be a joy, not a burden, for that would be of no advantage to you.

We saw this verse earlier when we talked about submission to spiritual authority. But does it make sense that, if you live under your parents' authority, this verse also applies to them? Read it through again, and just substitute the word **parents** for **leaders.** Is it starting to make sense?

I talk with a lot of parents of teenagers. People just like your parents. And do you know what they sometimes confide in me? ***Bringing you up is sometimes more of a burden for them than a joy!***

- **The way you behave when you get home from church**—*will it add to your parents' burdens or add to your parents' joy?*
- **The way you apply yourself at school or work this year**—*will it add to your parents' burdens or add to your parents' joy?*
- **The attitude you show to helping out around the house**—*will it add to your parents' burdens or add to your parents' joy?*

If I asked your parents—and they were honest with me—would they say that having you home made family life easier? Or would they say that having you home made it harder?

> Would they say that having you home made family life easier?

Will you obey your parents and submit to their authority? Will you obey your parents so that their parenting will be a joy and not a burden?

You can bring the most humungous change to your families by living as a totally transformed person with totally transformed submission. You can change from bringing your parents more burdens—to bringing them more joy. Sounds too hard? Remember that God has already given you everything you need to live like this!

Are you game to start?

TOTALLY

TRANSFORMED

SEX

14 The great gift of sex

I got an email from a friend recently. It was simply entitled "Cats".

CATS
1. They never consider how you feel. They do whatever they want no matter what you say.
2. When you want to be alone, they want to play. When you want to play, they want to be alone.
3. They are moody and irritable.
4. They complain loudly when they don't get their own way.
5. They leave little bits of their hair all around the house.

Conclusion: Cats are miniature women in fur coats.

Well, I thought that was funny and clever, and I was feeling a little superior until I received another email the next day, from the very same friend. It was simply entitled "Dogs".

DOGS
1. They lie around the house all day on the most comfortable piece of furniture.
2. They can hear a packet of food being opened half a block away—but they don't listen to you when you're in the same room as them.
3. When you want to play, they want to play. When you want to be alone, they want to play.
4. They can look both lovable and dumb at the same time.
5. They growl when they're not happy.
6. They leave their toys everywhere.

Conclusion: Dogs are miniature men in fur coats.

Hmm…

You see, somewhere along the line, you discovered that girls and guys were, well, just different.

When you were little kids in primary school, boys and girls sort of avoided each other. The girls played their girl games and the boys played their boy games. When I was a little boy, I steered clear of all those girls at school because I was scared of getting **girl-germs** … or **cooties** as they were eventually called.

All of us accepted this divided status—the world was a comfortable place for us—we were quite happy with our little rules. Until one day, some of the boys who were getting a little bit older, and a little bit bigger, started to notice that members of the opposite sex sort of had an attractive shape. A nice shape. An alluring shape…

"Like a toothpaste tube squeezed in all the right places…"

And as you entered your teens, you were suddenly attacked by that dreaded assailant— **puberty.** And everything changed! You discovered that you had a sexuality racing and throbbing through your body. All sorts of things were blossoming and developing. And the differences between guys and girls— you sort of worked out that you **liked** it! You were now starting to live life as a sexual being. It was all very new, very interesting, very enjoyable.

And then you discovered that the Bible had something to say about your sexuality. Maybe you thought that what God has to say was very negative. And maybe when you read the Bible about sex you felt guilty. And maybe when you read the Bible about sex you felt confused.

Because if you're not very careful, you can end up thinking that God is very negative about your sexuality. That somehow he doesn't like it very much. That somehow sex snuck in one day when God wasn't looking. That God sort of made Adam and Eve neutral, and one day turned around in horror and said: **"My goodness— what on earth are they doing?"**

As we look into the Bible, I want to show you that when God makes you a totally transformed person—he gives you a totally transformed sexuality. I want to show you from the Bible that the sexuality that God has placed in your body is absolutely fantastic, and God is very, very positive about it. God wants to give you the absolute best out of sex. As you read on, my prayer is that God will speak to you from the Bible and give you information about your sexuality that you will never get anywhere else.

This can be a difficult area for teenage Christians to be obedient in. Let's look together at God's word so that you will discover how to live out your sexuality in a totally transformed way. Let's go back to where it all started— the very first book of the Bible— **Genesis.**

GOD INVENTED SEX

Genesis 1:27
So God created man in his own image, in the image of God he created him; male and female he created them.

This is fantastic news! God has made you as a sexual person. He designed some of the human race to be male, and some to be female. **Yee-hah!** This means that the sexuality that throbs inside your body is something that God has designed, and God has invented, and God has placed within you. God designed you to be a sexual person.

GOD'S FIRST COMMAND

Have you ever figured out what God's first command to human beings was? That is, after he created us, what was the first thing that God wanted us to do? The most important thing he wanted to impress upon us. Don't look ahead. I want to know what you're thinking of. Are you thinking of a command which starts with the words *"Thou shalt not..."* ?

Let me show you what is the first command ever recorded in the Bible:

Genesis 1:28
God blessed them and said to them, "Be fruitful and increase in number; fill the earth and subdue it. Rule over the fish of the sea and the birds of the air and over every living creature that moves on the ground."

Did you catch that? God's first command to human beings is—to go and have sex—and have lots of it! *Serious?* **Yes!** Go back and read the passage to make sure I am not making this up! What does God mean: **"Be fruitful and increase in number"?** There's only one way that human beings can increase in number—by having sex to have more babies. God tells us to go and do that!

And how much sex does God want us to have? **"Fill the earth and subdue it!"** How could Adam and Eve have enough babies to **fill the earth** ? Only one way to achieve that— **have lots and lots of sex!**

YOUR SEXUALITY IS VERY GOOD

You see, God invented sexuality. He gave it to you as a special gift. He said: **"I want you to go and use it. I want you to enjoy it."**

Sex is not a bad thing. God didn't give it to you just to frustrate the heck out of you. God didn't give you your sexuality to make life painful and difficult. God says that your sexuality is **very good.** He **wants** you to have it!

Have a look back through Genesis Chapter 1. It's a description of how God created everything. God's creation is described as taking place over six days. And on most days, there is a summary verse that is repeated.

Genesis 1:3-4
And God said, "Let there be light," and there was light. God saw that the light was good …"

"God saw that the light was good …" that's the little phrase I meant. God looks down on what he has just made, and he sees that it is **good.** The same phrase is there when God creates the land and sea (verse 10), trees (verse 12), the sun and the moon (verse 18), the fish and the birds (verse 21), and the animals (verse 25). It's good. God thinks it's brilliant.

At the end of creation, just after God has made man and woman, just after he has created us as sexual beings, we read the following statement:

> **Genesis 1:31**
> *God saw all that he had made, and it was **very good...***

Not just good — brilliant

God looked down at everything he had made—including your sexuality—and God concluded that it was **very good.**

So—if everything that God creates is **good,** what is the first thing in the Bible that God says is **not good?**

"IT IS NOT GOOD"

> **Genesis 2:18**
> *The LORD God said, "It is not good for the man to be alone. I will make a helper suitable for him.*

When God looks down and sees that he has made a man—but there is no partner for him—and the man is alone—God concludes: **"It is not good for the man to be alone."**

It's as if God is saying: **"I have a design for this universe which is not yet completed. I have designed my human beings for relationships. The man is alone—that is not good."**

THE IDEAL PARTNER

We then read an almost comical version of how God makes a whole series of creatures who might indeed be the ideal partner for the lonely man. As God makes each creature, he brings it to the man for the man to name.

Genesis 2:19-20

Now the LORD God had formed out of the ground all the beasts of the field and all the birds of the air. He brought them to the man to see what he would name them; and whatever the man called each living creature, that was its name. So the man gave names to all the livestock, the birds of the air and all the beasts of the field. But for Adam **no suitable helper was found.**

You can imagine the scene: God makes a new creature and brings it to the man.

"Well Adam, what do you think? I've made a brand new creature here. What shall we call it?"

"Let's call it a cow!"

"Nice name, Adam! 'Cow' it is then! So, what do you think of this 'cow'?"

"That's really nice God, but it's not quite what I'm looking for in a life-long partner."

Adam called me a pig!

God makes another creature.

"What about this one, Adam?"

"Let's call it an eagle!"

"Okay, Adam! 'Eagle' it is then! So, what do you think of it?

"That's really nice, Lord, but when I said I was looking for a bird…"

You get the point. Every one of God's creations was fantastic, but no matter how spectacular and special they were, the conclusion of verse 20 states: **"But for Adam no suitable helper was found."**

Genesis 2:22-23

Then the LORD God made a woman from the rib he had taken out of the man, and he brought her to the man. The man said, "This is now bone of my bones and flesh of my flesh; she shall be called 'woman', for she was taken out of man."

God brings this final fantastic creature to Adam, and his reaction is very different from his response to any of the other creatures God has brought to him. You can almost hear Adam crying out with delight: **"Whoa!!!! This one is a beauty, God! You have excelled yourself! I couldn't think of a more ideal partner! Way to go! Let's call her 'Woman'!"**

God makes men—and God makes women. And he makes us for a relationship with each other. And personally—I rather agree with Adam that it is a **brilliant** idea!

A COMMITTED UNION

Have you got the main point? God's first command is: **"Go and have sex and have lots of it!"**

But just before you race out in obedience to God to explore every part of your sexuality, you also need to understand that the inventor of your sexuality gives us careful guidelines on how to use it. God wants you to get the absolute best out of sex. It is an absolutely brilliant gift from God, and he wants you to enjoy it to the absolute max. So God gives you a careful framework so you will get the absolute best out of sex.

Genesis 2:24

For this reason a man will leave his father and mother and be united to his wife, and they will become one flesh.

GOD'S THREE GUIDELINES

Here is a summary of everything that God says about sex in the Bible. These are the guidelines he has laid in place so that you can enjoy sex the most. Here is the structure he has put in place to safeguard his beautiful gift of sex, and to safeguard everyone who gets involved sexually. Now look back at Genesis 2:24, and see where these three guidelines come from.

1. A man and a woman

God designed sexual activity to take place between **a man and a woman.** The teaching from the Bible on this subject is clear. God did not give us our sexuality for two women to enjoy together; he did not give us our sexuality for two men to enjoy together; he didn't even give you your sexuality so you can enjoy it all by yourself in a corner.

God's first guideline—sexual activity is to take place between a man and a woman.

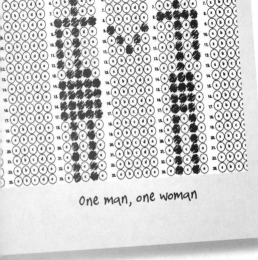

one man, one woman

As you are growing towards maturity as the person God made you—you will struggle with different feelings. The teenage years can be a bit confusing. The fact that you get tempted to use your sexuality in a certain way doesn't mean you have to be locked into using it that way for the rest of your life. It's okay to talk about it. And a Christian community—a church, a Christian youth group, or a Bible-study group—is a great place to talk about it. We need to help each other to get it right, and support each other when we get it wrong.

Now for Guideline Number Two:

2. In a one-to-one...

It's not meant to be one guy sleeping with any girl he can get. It's not meant to be a girl sleeping with any guy who will have her. In the biblical view, sex is not a group activity. It is a special relationship between one man and one woman—and it is not to be shared with anyone else.

Now for Guideline Number Three:

3. Committed, lifelong relationship

God's plan is not to have one guy committing to a girl—and then changing his mind and getting another sexual partner. It's not living together until you get tired of each other. It's not *"try before you buy",* where you go sexually exploring a large range of partners until you find one who meets your high standards. God wants sexuality to be used within the safety of a committed lifelong relationship. Where both partners are committed to each other—for life—no matter what.

Within that framework, God wants sex to be a huge blessing for you. That is God's way to use sex. That is the **moral** way to use your sexuality. If you use sex **outside** God's guidelines, it is called **sexual immorality.** Something which is immoral is something which is against the morals of God; something which is against the design of God; something against the magnificence that God wants you to have in your sexuality.

Sexual immorality is any sexual activity that falls outside Gods guidelines of…

- a man and a woman…
- in a one-to-one…
- committed, lifelong relationship…

So here's the big question: **"How far can I go"?** Or to express it in another way: **"If I'm going to be an obedient Christian, how much sexual immorality is okay?"**

Next chapter!

15 Not even a hint

*Here's the big question: if anything that lies outside God's guidelines for sex is called **sexual immorality**, if I'm going to be an obedient Christian, how much sexual immorality is okay?*

Here's the answer:

> ### Ephesians 5:3
> *But among you there must be not even a hint of sexual immorality, or of any kind of impurity, or of greed, because these are improper for God's holy people.*

Did you catch that? **Not even a hint!** The Bible says that even a **hint** of sexual immorality is out of character for the person who wants to follow Jesus.

Not even a hint? **Serious?**

Right now you might be thinking: **"I don't want to hear this!"** There must be something better on sex than this. I didn't buy this book just to be told that sex is only for marriage. Are you seriously saying that if I'm exploring and experimenting and playing around—that's wrong?"

> *"I don't want to hear this stuff! I want to hear from someone else about sex!"*

Okay. I understand that. But who else are you going to listen to?

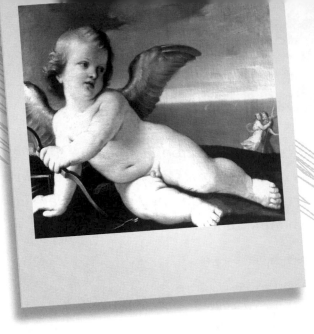

Everything you read in the Bible is a carefully crafted word from God—a guiding word from the supreme being who created your sexuality, who designed your sexuality and who loves you intensely. **Who else are you going to listen to?**

Do you want an alternative point of view? What about these words from *Clothes Off* by *Gym Class Heroes*:

> *"So here's the thing…*
> *We have to take our clothes off, we have to party all night*
> *We have to take our clothes off, to have a good time*
> *(you're so sexy)."*

Does that give you a better framework to use your precious gift of sexuality? Does that guide you better as to how to have deep and lasting relationships with others?

What about this offering from *Cupid's Chokehold*—also sung by *Gym Class Heroes* (reviving the *Supertramp* song):

> *Take a look at my girlfriend, girlfriend,*
> *She's the only one I got.*
> *Not much of a girlfriend, girlfriend*
> *I never seem to get a lot.*

Is that going to help you live a strong and satisfied life? Is that better advice than what God gives? If you don't like God's guidelines, would you like to take your clues from *The Bad Touch*—by *The Bloodhound Gang?*

> *You and me baby ain't nothing but mammals*
> *So lets do it like they do on the Discovery Channel*

Well, there's a great attitude to sex! Let's just go hammer and tongs! Let's just do it—*Wham! Bam! Thank You Ma'am!*

Here's the problem: You might well know the devastation of having someone *"do it to you like they do on the Discovery Channel."* Perhaps you have been crushed by someone like that. Someone who just used you.

Maybe you're still in a relationship where someone is just *doing it to you.* You know the emptiness that goes with that. You know the awfulness where the beauty is taken away from sexuality and you've just got the leftovers.

> *"Let's do it like they do on the Discovery Channel"*

Maybe you are in relationship like that. Maybe you're doing it to someone like that. It might only be what you think about. You might only dream and imagine that you're doing it to someone *"like they do on the Discovery Channel."*

Rush 'em, mush 'em, crush 'em and flush 'em

The world doesn't need a sexuality that says: *"Do just what you feel like."* You know there are all sorts of people who'll just use sex simply for their own benefit. It won't be anything to do with purity. It won't be anything to do with giving. It won't be anything to do with love. It will be just to do with greed because that's what they can get for themselves.

You know there are people who will treat others like that. You know how some guys operate on girls. They use the **"rush 'em, mush 'em, crush 'em and flush 'em"** approach. They rush in on some vulnerable girl; pounce on them with fake romance; crush them in the process, and then flush them away like garbage at the end. Girls and guys sometimes use each other like some new video game. They put their money in the slot; they play the game for all they're worth; they keep trying until they achieve top score;

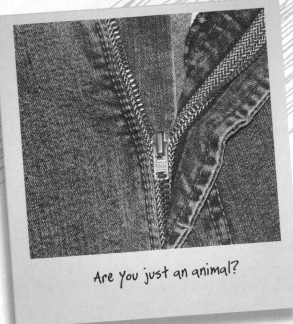

Are you just an animal?

and then they just lose interest. They abandon that game and race on to something new that shines with the promise of more excitement.

You've probably met those super-studs who just have girls hanging off every word they say. They attract girls like flies… they treat girls like flies… and they've got their brains in their flies!

Are you just a mammal? Are you just the same as any other animal? Do you just respond to any urging that you happen to feel? And if you do just respond to any instinct that you feel, **what do you think of yourself?**

Are you really nothing but a mammal? Isn't there something that separates you from the rest of the animal kingdom? God doesn't look down at you and see someone who's **just a mammal.** He doesn't see you as someone who is the same as any other animal, in a slightly more intelligent form.

God looks down at you and he says: **"I made you. I crafted you. I put you together. I knitted you together in your mother's womb. You are fearfully and wonderfully made. That's who you are."**

"And I sent my son to be butchered on a cross for you. I cared that much about you that I called you back. You're not just some animal in my sight. You're my son. You're my daughter. I love you."

So if you're just **"doing it like they do on the Discovery Channel"** —what do you think about yourself? God says: **"I have something far better in mind for you. You are much more special to me than you could ever imagine."**

Even though you know all this to be true, your whole body will sometimes send you a different message. If you're a teenager, with all sorts of hormones running uncontrolled throughout your entire body, it's very easy to feel: **"But you don't understand! You don't understand what it's like being in my body. I have these overwhelming urges. I've just got to do it!"**

You might even end up saying:

> *"God has given me these overwhelming urges. Surely God wouldn't let me have these urges unless he wants me to fulfil them?"*

Let me now introduce you to something brilliant that God has given each and every one of you. It is something utterly brilliant and precious, and many people spend their whole lives not realising they have it.

You have the power to make a choice!

16 The power to make a choice

One of the things that marks you out from the animal kingdom is that you have the power to make a choice. You're not just controlled by instincts. You get to make decisions. You get to make a choice.

THE ABILITY TO CHOOSE

1 Thessalonians 4:3-4
It is God's will that you should be sanctified: that you should avoid sexual immorality; that each of you should learn to control his own body in a way that is holy and honourable...

You don't have to be governed by the urges and the instincts you have. As God's person you have the ability to **learn to control your own body.**

You have already learned that. Imagine you are sitting in class at school. You become aware of being uncomfortable. You realise that your bladder is getting fuller and fuller. You are being struck with an overwhelming urge to empty it. The urge keeps getting stronger and stronger. You feel that if you don't act on this urge, your whole body will explode.

My hope is that you have learned how to control your own body. Even though your bladder is sending through a strong message: **"Empty me now! Release the tension immediately!",** I suspect that you don't just sit there in class and empty your bladder everywhere! You have learned to control and delay the urges and instincts in your body. You have learned to hold back when it is not proper for your body to do something that it is screaming at you to do. You wait for a more appropriate time. You wait for a more appropriate place.

You might feel as if your whole body is about to explode

With your sexuality it is exactly the same. You might well feel strong sexual urges within your body. Your body will scream at you that you must release these tensions **now!** You might feel as if your whole body will explode if you don't give in to these sexual urges.

I have some good news for you. I have investigated this carefully. In every known case where the police have investigated a suspicious death of a teenager, they have **never once** recorded their findings as **"This person exploded and died because they did not release their sexual tension"!** Your body might be screaming at you that you will explode and die if you don't give in to your sexual urges, **but your body is lying to you. You don't have to give in to every urge in your body. God has given you the power to make a choice!**

God says:

> "I have designed you with the ability to make decisions. You're not going to be controlled by the circumstances around you. And you're not going to be controlled by the person whom you're with. And you're not going to be controlled by your urges and your instincts. You're not going to be controlled by the things you're taking into you because you're getting drunk. You are going to be controlled by the Spirit of God and make the choices to say 'yes' to Jesus and 'no' to ungodliness."

That is a choice that you are able to make. Do you trust God enough to keep making it?

So let's just check again… with sexual immorality… How far is too far? How much is too much?

> **Ephesians 5:3**
> But among you there must be not even a hint of sexual
> immorality, or of any kind of impurity, or of greed, because these
> are improper for God's holy people.

How many porno websites can I look at? I mean —it's only a photo… it's only a video. No-one gets hurt. How much of that can I do and still claim to be following Jesus?

God says: *"Not even a hint."*

So when I'm with my girlfriend or boyfriend. I mean, we're not going to "do it". We're not going all the way. We're just going to fool around and explore, you know, experiment with each other, a bit of looking and groping…

How much exploring can we do? How much groping can we do? How much looking under clothing can we do? How much feeling around can we do and still be honouring Jesus?

God says: *"Not even a hint."*

When I'm at school or with my friends, how much flirting can I do? Can I have a little bit on the side? How much sexual innuendo can I have?

God says: *"Not even a hint."*

Does it matter what jokes that I listen to? Does it matter if I tell dirty stories? Does it matter if I make some fun out of the sexuality bit? Can I just degrade a few people, ridicule them and treat them like dirt because it's **so funny?**

God says: *"Not even a hint."*

Does it matter if there's a person that I'm seeing now that I shouldn't really be seeing? Does it matter that I'm stepping outside a marriage relationship? Does it matter that there's a person that no one else knows about and no damage is being done and we're enjoying life and no one else knows?

God says: *"Not even a hint."*

What about the guilt that I feel when I'm doing things I shouldn't be doing? And I keep doing it even though I know it's wrong! I know that as a Christian I should be taking a stand, but the pressure is so great, and I don't know how to say "no", and I want to look cool with everybody else, and I don't want to be thought of as a weirdo with old-fashioned ideas, so I just join in stuff that I know is wrong…

God could not be clearer:

> **Ephesians 5:3**
> *But among you there must be not even a hint of sexual immorality, or of any kind of impurity, or of greed, because these are improper for God's holy people.*

KNOWING GOD'S FORGIVENESS

It's exciting that God calls us to a totally transformed level of faithfulness. God wants you to have a level of obedience that honours him in every single area of your life so there's **not even a hint** that you're dishonouring him.

Maybe you know that God's hand is upon you and God is saying: "Something has to change". Something you're thinking. Something you're saying. Something you're doing. Maybe you have become aware that in some area of your life there is at least **a hint** of sexual immorality.

Is God saying to you: **"There are things that have to change in your life. You can no longer go on pretending."** Maybe you've worked out that in some areas of your life there is **more** than a hint!

Here is the good news. If you truly are following Jesus—if you genuinely

You have the option

want to live for him—then that means, whenever you fail him, **he has already died for that sin.**

He loves to see his people realise when they are wrong—and turn back to him.

As far as the east is from the west, so far has he removed our transgressions from us

Psalm 103:11-13
For as high as the heavens are above the earth, so great is his love for those who fear him; as far as the east is from the west, so far has he removed our transgressions from us. As a father has compassion on his children, so the LORD has compassion on those who fear him...

If you truly have become a Christian, if you are honestly trusting your whole life to Jesus' death—then this promise is for you. Try reading these verses from Psalm 103 again—but this time make it personal, and put your own name in there.

Psalm 103:11-13 (personalised)
For as high as the heavens are above the earth, so great is God's love for me; as far as the east is from the west, so far has he removed my transgressions from me. As a father has compassion on his children, so the LORD has compassion on me.

If you genuinely want to come back to Jesus—if you want to turn away from every sin—if you want to turn away from every **sexual** sin—then answer this question: *"If Jesus has died for me, what has happened to my sexual sin?"* The answer is there in verse 12: *"As far as the east is from the west, so far has God removed my sins from me".*

There may be some work for you to do. There may be some sins that you need to intentionally turn away from. There may be a relationship you need to pull out of; or a hard disk to erase; or magazines to burn; or web-pages to remove from your **favourites** tab; there might be some tough decisions for you to take, but here is something that is clear: **God loves to see his people turn back to him.**

There are **four decisions** which will really help you if you want to turn away from any sin:

- **Decide to turn away from that sin.** Decide to give it up completely.
- **Decide to turn back to God.** Immerse yourself in him—in his word—in prayer—in worship.
- **Decide to remove the area of temptation** where you are most likely to stumble.
- **Decide to make yourself accountable** to a Christian friend or leader.

In the past week, two young Christian men in their late teens approached me to help them deal with sin. For one of them, the big decision he had to make was to erase an entire hard drive full of filthy images. For the other one, he had to decide to install software on his computer which will automatically send me an email if he visits any erotic websites.

Do you see what they were doing? They weren't just deciding to turn away from sin and to turn back to God *(Decisions 1 and 2)*. Both these decisions they could carry out by themselves. But they took the hard step. Each one of them made the difficult decision to remove the temptation *(Decision 3)*, and make themselves accountable to me *(Decision 4)*. If there's a sin you need to turn away from—don't try to avoid it all alone! Let a trusted Christian brother or sister walk with you so they can help you and support you.

The off switch is less messy...

Don't to go back to being the person you used to be! Keep pressing on to become the person that God **wants** you to be!

God's promise is faithful:

Isaiah 1:18

Though your sins are like scarlet, they shall be as white as snow; though they are red as crimson, they shall be like wool.

God's forgiveness is so big. His love is so big. He wants you to be his faithful follower.

If God is putting his hand on you now—to say there is at least a hint of sexual immorality in the relationship you're in… in what you're saying… in what you're thinking… in what you're looking at… in what you're lusting after… what are you going to do about it?

Will you make that change now? Will you make yourself accountable to another Christian now? Will you determine to live a new and pure life now? That choice might seem terrifyingly hard—almost impossible. But remember that God has already given you everything you need to be a totally transformed person.

Are you prepared to have your sexuality **totally transformed?**

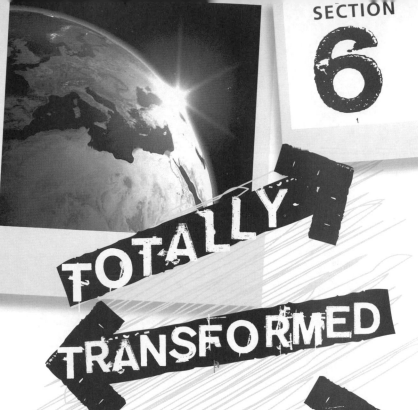

SECTION 6

TOTALLY

TRANSFORMED

MISSION

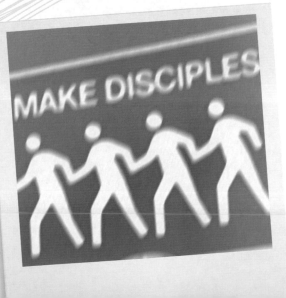

MAKE DISCIPLES

17 You've changed kingdoms

*Imagine that you join some sort of protest group. You want to make a stand for a worthwhile cause. Let's say that you join **Greenpeace**. But instantly you discover a problem. You now have a completely new set of values...*

THE PROBLEM OF BEING DIFFERENT

You want to make a stand for things that once never bothered you. And you want to help stacks of your friends to see things in a new way as well. But you don't want to be thought of as a weirdo. And you don't want to compromise your values.

If you're not careful, there are three problem areas that you might well find yourself in.

PROBLEM 1 – HOLDING BACK

You don't want to hang around with people who mistreat animals. So you hang out with all the other greenies. You have great meetings. You get involved in a lot of environmental activities. You don't really want to spend time with all those environmental destroyers out there— and you find that the organisation keeps you so busy that you don't really have **time** to spend with outsiders.

It all **seems** as if it's going okay, but every now and again, you wonder:

> *"If I never have any contact with outsiders, how will we ever get any more Greenpeace members?*
> *How will we spread the message to more and more people?"*

PROBLEM 2 – SHUTTING UP

Now that you've joined *Greenpeace*, you still maintain your old friendships. Indeed, you make it top priority to link up with outsiders. But you don't want them to think you're a weirdo. So you decide that you won't mention the word *Greenpeace*. You make sure that you don't talk about any environmental issues with them. I mean, you don't want to turn them off by being too pushy!

So you keep quiet. But there's the problem. How will you convince outsiders to join your cause if you never say anything?

PROBLEM 3 – GIVING IN

You realise your friends sort of know that you've joined *Greenpeace*. But you don't want them treating you any differently. You want to show them that you're just a regular person. So you keep going with them on their hunting expeditions. *"You're not scared to club a baby seal to death—are you?"*

Big problem! How do you make a stand for the environment when you keep joining in wrong stuff with your friends?

BEING A CHRISTIAN AMONG NON-CHRISTIANS.

Sometimes it can be hard making a stand for Jesus in a world that does not care very much about him. You don't want to compromise your values, so you tend to hang out with Christians all the time. But you want to reach others—so you start hanging out with them—but you're scared to say anything. And in your effort to appear to be **just a normal person,** you might even end up joining in with your friends when they do things that are disobedient to God.

These are the three traps that it is so easy to fall into:

- **Holding back**—you just hang around with Christians all the time, *or*
- **Shutting up**—you keep quiet about your faith, *or*
- **Giving in**—you join in the wrong things your friends do.

The devil will use these three methods to keep Christians away from the central job that Jesus has given us to do. Before Jesus left, he said: **_"Go and make disciples"._** That is the one mission—the one task—that he has left for us to do. To help other people to discover the life-changing message about Jesus that has transformed your own life. Without holding back. Without shutting up. Without giving in.

God has made you to be a totally transformed person. He has now given you a totally transformed mission in life—to help totally transform your friends.

How can you be a faithful and effective Christian when you're around your non-Christian friends? How can you avoid the problems of holding back... shutting up... or giving in? There's a great passage in Ephesians 5:8-16 which answers all these questions. Let's check it out!

YOU HAVE MOVED FROM DARKNESS TO LIGHT

Ephesians 5:8a

For you were once darkness, but now you are light in the Lord...

1. You were once darkness but now you are light

If you've become a Christian, then you've changed sides. The Bible says that when you decided to follow Jesus, God rescued you out of the kingdom of darkness and moved you into the kingdom of light.

You might have thought that when you became a Christian, it was just a little step. Just a small change of heart. Just a tiny decision.

No! No! No! When you made the decision to follow Jesus, you were transferred out of one kingdom and into another. You moved out of the

kingdom of darkness and into the kingdom of light. You moved out of the kingdom that was following Satan, and you moved into the kingdom that was following Jesus. That's why Jesus' death on the cross was such a big deal!

This is what God has done for all who turn to Jesus:

Colossians 1:13

For he has rescued us from the dominion of darkness and brought us into the kingdom of the Son he loves.

This world might not seem that dark to you. But when people cut themselves off from the light of Christ—they live in

When people cut themselves off from the light of Christ they live in darkness.

darkness. They live in a world with no light. They live in a world with no way forward. They live in a world with no future.

And that's the world you used to be in before you came to Jesus.

2. So live as a child of the light!

Ephesians 5:8b

"For you were once darkness, but now you are light in the Lord. Live as children of light...

God says in the Bible: **"If you've moved into the kingdom of light—stop living as if you're still in darkness!"**

Imagine what it would be like to live in a world of total darkness. No sun. No street lights. There are no torches and no candles. You'd need to work out ways of coping. You would walk very slowly. Very carefully. You'd stay huddled together with family and friends. You couldn't take any risks.

If it was totally dark—no one could see you—you could do what you liked—and no one would notice. You wouldn't have to brush your hair—no-one would ever see it. You wouldn't have to smile at people. You

stop living as if you're still
in the darkness

wouldn't have to wear clothes. No one would know! You see, when no one can see you—you get up to all sorts of crazy things!

Ephesians 5 tells us—if God has rescued you out of the kingdom of darkness—and placed you in the kingdom of light—then stop living as if you're still in the darkness!

Imagine living in the kingdom of light—and still living as if you were in total darkness! Walking very slowly. Staying huddled together. Not taking any risks. Not bothering to brush your hair. Not bothering to wear your clothes. Acting like no one can see you.

It's crazy! Imagine living in a world of light, but still living like you were in total darkness! And yet that's sometimes what we do as Christians.

In fact, there's one more important step:

3. Find out what pleases the Lord

Ephesians 5:10

Live as children of light … and find out what pleases the Lord.

That's why we're looking at the Bible now. That's why you spend time in prayer. That's why you gather together with other Christians. You do all this so you can find out what pleases the Lord.

Imagine you get a new boyfriend or girlfriend. It's a great new relationship—and it means so much to both of you. But you just keep doing your own thing. You never bother finding out what your partner wants to do—you just keep doing stuff that **you** enjoy. When it is their birthday, you don't bother finding out what **they'd** like—you simply buy them a present that **you'd** like. You have no idea about their interests, their hobbies, their taste in music, what sport they like—or whether indeed they like sport at all. You're simply not interested in whether they're attracted to or disgusted by your little personal habits. You don't ever find out what delights them or what bores them. You ignore their interests altogether and insist that they simply join in what **you** like doing.

Can you imagine that? If you continued on like this, I can assure you—your relationship has no future—and your future has no relationship!

Exactly the same is true with your relationship with Jesus. Imagine becoming a Christian, and just continuing on with everything you've always done without ever checking **"Does this please Jesus?"** Is it possible that there are some things that you are currently doing in your life that maybe Jesus is not pleased with at all?

So what should you do about the things that belong to the old kingdom of darkness?

Next chapter!

Use your light to change the darkness

Ephesians 5:11

Have nothing to do with the fruitless deeds of darkness ...

Anything which hides the light of Christ is a fruitless deed of darkness. It will never achieve anything. It will only take you away from Jesus.

When your friends are saying: "Let's miss school today", that is a fruitless deed of darkness. When everyone agrees to lie to their parents about going to a party, that is a fruitless deed of darkness.

The list is endless! When everyone's making fun of someone who's different... when other kids have DVDs and magazines which degrade God's great gift of sex... when your mates are taking stuff out of the shop without paying for it... when those around you are vandalising or destroying someone's property... when your sporting team is using dirty tactics to take out the opposition... when your mates are getting drunk or stoned... when people are using their

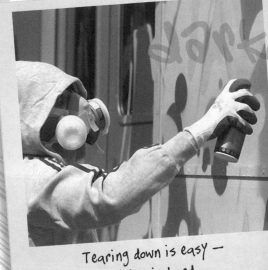

Tearing down is easy — building is hard ...

sexuality to harass others… when smart comments are being yelled out at the teacher in class… when your friends in church are just distracting everyone and dishonouring Jesus by their behaviour…

Whatever it is, the Bible says: **"Have nothing to do with the fruitless deeds of darkness".** Get rid of them absolutely.

Remember what we learned in Chapter 3?

> ### Ephesians 4:22-24
> *Put off your old self, which is being corrupted by its deceitful desires … be made new in the attitude of your minds … put on the new self, created to be like God in true righteousness and holiness.*

This verse reminds us that when we start a new life with Jesus, he gives us a whole new way to live. It's like getting rid of a set of old stinking clothes, and replacing them with a set of brand new clothes.

Remember the two problems?

1. Don't leave your old clothes on

You start to take your old stinking clothes off… but then you realise you like them… so you leave them on.

Just dump it …

Then you try to put the purity of Jesus right over the top of your rotten, stinking deeds of darkness! And you wonder why you're not doing that well at obeying Jesus!

2. Don't leave your old clothes in the wardrobe

Sometimes rather than throwing away your rotten, stinking, old clothes, and burning them in the incinerator, you take them off—but you hang them in the wardrobe. Just so they're handy. Just in case you need them. Just in case your new clothes don't work out. Just in case you decide to take your new clothes back to the store.

Sometimes you will be tempted to do that. You will put on the brand new life that Jesus offers… you take off your old ways of darkness… but you leave your sins and temptation really handy in your spiritual wardrobe! Ready to go back to if the Christian bit doesn't satisfy you any more. Ready to put on if you get sick of this new Christian life.

You see, if you're serious about giving up angry words—don't leave them there in your wardrobe so you can use them any time you need them. Get rid of them! If you're serious about not visiting those porno websites—then take them out of your favourites and put a filter on so you can't go back to them! If you're serious about living the brand new life of Jesus—don't hang on to your deeds of darkness.

Maybe today is the day that you get rid of something completely.

USE YOUR LIGHT TO CHANGE THE DARKNESS

Ephesians 5:11
Have nothing to do with the fruitless deeds of darkness, but rather expose them.

Imagine your friends still live in a world of darkness. They live in a world ruled by fear. And they do whatever they want.

Wouldn't it be crazy to go back to living that way! Just joining in with your friends in the stupid things they're doing. If your friends are in darkness, and you've got a light that would help them… what sort of a friend are you if you keep the light to yourself?

Ephesians 5:11
Have nothing to do with the fruitless deeds of darkness, but rather expose them.

Don't judge your friends. Don't condemn them for what they're doing. But simply say: **"I don't need to live that way any more. I've found something better."**

Many years ago when I was a much younger youth pastor—with much freakier hair (indeed—with much **more** hair!)—I did a lot of work on the streets in my local area. I would cruise around the shopping centre looking to build relationships that I had started with students at school.

It might have had something to do with what I looked like, but often people on the streets would try and sell me drugs. How did I respond to that? I desperately wanted to use my light to challenge their darkness. So I said:

> "No thanks—I don't need that any more.
> I've got something much better!"

Then I would move away. Often they used to follow me. *"What do you mean, you've got something better?"* I would reply: *"You wouldn't be interested!"* and keep moving away. Sometimes they would end up chasing me—begging me to tell them what I had that was better than what they had. Then—and only then—would I tell them about the Lord who gave me life.

If you're going to take the light of Jesus and shine it in the world of darkness, you have to be prepared to cop some garbage. People will always throw rubbish at you. But you don't have to grab it and rub your face in it!

BRING YOUR FRIENDS TO THE LIGHT

Ephesians 5:15-16
Be very careful, then, how you live—not as unwise but as wise, making the most of every opportunity, because the days are evil.

Make the most of every opportunity. Don't let a chance go by where you could lead your friends to discover the difference that Jesus can make.

If you really want to take the most of every opportunity… if you really have a passion to have nothing to do with the deeds of darkness… if you desperately want to reach out to your friends and bring them to the light of Christ… if you really understand what this **transformed mission** is all about—then you might need to take some very bold and courageous steps.

Scott was a student in our youth ministry. He came from a Christian family and had been growing strongly as a Christian for some years. He came along to the youth group I ran; he was always there at church; and he was a keen participant in his weekly Bible study. He had been a student at the local

Christian school for the last four years—he had two more years of schooling to go—and he was on track to be appointed as a house captain at his Christian school.

He was at the point in his life where he was making decisions about his final two years of high school. He came to me and said: *"I want to transfer to the local state high school."* I tried to find out whether there were any problems at his current, rather nice Christian school, but no, he was doing well there, and enjoying it. He was surrounded by a large circle of good Christian friends, and was very comfortable in his Christian school environment.

He explained it to me:

> *"There are some guys in my grade from the high school who came on our youth group camp. They seemed interested in Jesus, but there's no one at their school to help and encourage them. I want to move to help bring students to Christ!"*

A bold vision—a bold heart—and a bold decision. Scott made that move from the comfort of the Christian school to the mission field of the public school. The result? There has been a steady stream of people from that school visiting our youth group and camps. And yes—there is a small number who have now made the commitment to follow Jesus!

That's a totally transformed mission!

Here's the problem. As soon as you read about bringing your friends to Christ, you probably think: **"But how do I do it? How can I bring my friends to Jesus?"**

Read on to discover four easy steps!

Four steps to bring your friends to Christ

When Jesus called you to follow him, as well as giving you a totally transformed way to live, he also gave you a totally transformed mission. He has given you a task to do—and empowered you with his Spirit so that you will be able to do it. Jesus wants you to be part of his team, that calls the rest of the world to follow him.

The rest of the world? Yes! When Jesus was empowering his followers just before he ascended back to heaven, he said to them:

> **Matthew 28:19**
> *Go and make disciples of all nations...*

If you are a follower of Jesus, you get to be a world-changer! You get to alter the destiny of nations! You get to grow and expand the kingdom of God here on earth. And how does the Kingdom of God grow? **One life at a time!**

Who is that **one life** that you can start to influence? Who is that **one colleague** that you can share something of your Christian life with? Who is that **one friend** who you can invite to your Christian youth group?

So how do I do that? Here are four easy steps to help you have a totally transformed mission. Check these out—these are steps that **anyone** can do. We call it being a **P-E-E-R** witness.

Here are the four steps:

- **P**ray
- **E**ncourage
- **E**vangelise
- **R**ecruit

STEP 1 - PRAY

Simply write down the names of three of your friends who are not yet Christians. Three friends—of the same gender as you—and approximately the same age as you. Three friends—who might go to your school—or play in your sporting team—or that you can easily mix with on a day-to-day basis.

All you do now is commit yourself to pray daily for them. And don't just pray that God would bring them to become a Christian. Pray that God would use **you** to help them become a Christian! A much bolder prayer!

Can you do that? Simply pray for your three unsaved friends every day? It might seem like a straightforward step, but imagine that if every Christian was doing this—faithfully—daily, then the world would be changed!

STEP 2 - ENCOURAGE

Now for each of those three friends whom you are praying for each day, look out for opportunities to personally encourage each one. How can you get alongside each one and meet them at a real point

simply pray for your three friends every day

of need? Invite them over? Hang out with them? Help them in some practical way? Random acts of kindness? All you are doing is showing Christ's love to them. Simple—but powerful!

Don't freak out!

Don't freak out at the word **evangelise!** All it means is that at some stage you need to say something about your faith. If you don't use some words to explain what you're doing, all your random acts of kindness might just make it look as if you're a **nice guy.** So... how do I say something about my faith?

Try these five **baby steps** of evangelism:

1. Tell them you go to your Christian youth group

That's it! As you're catching up at school on Monday, and you're asking each other what you did over the weekend, just include…

> *"I went to my youth group and we had a great discussion about…"*

That's it. You don't need any more at the moment. Just let them know you go to a Christian youth group (or any other Christian activity you attend).

2. Tell them you go to church

Easy! Same as above! At some stage in your conversation, just let your friend know that you go to church. Simple!

3. Tell them that you're a Christian

When there's an opportunity, let your friend know that you've decided to follow Jesus. Let them know that being a Christian is making a difference to your life. It could be as simple as...

> *"Since I've become a Christian, I've changed my mind about that."*

All you are doing is introducing into the conversation that you follow Jesus.

4. Give them one reason why

At some stage, give your friend **one reason** why you are a Christian. You don't have to give them **every** reason. You don't even have to give them the most **important** reason. Just **one** reason.

> *"Since I've become a Christian I have a real purpose to my life."*

> *"I get huge support from my fellow Christians to help me with the hassles I am facing."*

Just one reason!

5. Ask them if they're interested

> *"You know this Christian stuff that I talk about—have you ever been interested in that?"*

Even as you read these words, there are potentially two big fears that are rising up within you:

Fear Number One—What if they say "no"?

The devil always suggests this to us. ***"Don't say anything about Jesus! It might turn them off! What if they say 'no'?"*** You need to see this lie for all it's worth. **Your friend will not say "yes" unless you ask them!** That is, they're already saying "no" before you ask them. So if they say "no" after you ask them, you haven't lost anything. And remember—they're not saying **"No—never!"** They're saying **"No—not now!"**

So go on—it's okay to ask. It's okay for you to ask a friend a question and for your friend to say "no". They won't hit you! They won't end your friendship! They're just saying **"No—not now!"**

Fear Number Two—What if they say "yes"?

If your friend says: *"Well actually, I am interested in that stuff about Jesus"*, what are you going to say? What are you going to do?

Quite simple, really— **go to Step Four!**

STEP 4 - RECRUIT

Simply invite your friend along to an activity where they will find out more about Jesus.

> *"Hey—why don't I pick you up and bring you to my youth group on Friday night?"*

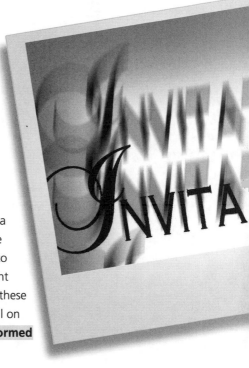

You don't have to do it all by yourself. There are stacks of Christians back at your church who can help you. That's how the body of Christ works!

Can you do these four steps? One at a time? There's no rush. There's no time limit. It might take you four minutes to work through all four steps, or it might take you four months. But if you put these four steps into action, you will be well on your way to having a **totally transformed mission.**

TOTALLY
TRANSFORMED
LIFE

20 From death to life

If you have made it this far—well done! You may have a mixture of feelings about what you've read so far in this book. Excitement at the challenge to live a totally transformed life... a bit frightened perhaps about the changes that will have to take place... or maybe despair that the life that Jesus calls you to is something that seems completely impossible to you right now. If that's how you're feeling, then these final two chapters are just for you...

I heard a story about a man who used to take a shortcut home each night. Instead of walking all the way around the block, he would take a shortcut through the town cemetery. One night—it was very dark—and as he took his usual shortcut through the cemetery, he did not notice that the workmen had dug a fresh grave, ready for a burial the next morning. In the darkness of the night, he slipped and fell straight into this freshly dug grave.

His first thought was to try and get out, but he was quite a short man, and he could not reach up to ground level. Every time he jumped up to try and

haul himself out, he merely slipped back down—stuck in this empty grave. He yelled and called out for some time, but eventually he realised that he would have to wait until morning to be rescued. So he lay down in a corner of the grave, put his thick, dark coat over himself for protection, and promptly fell asleep.

A little later that night, another man was taking the same shortcut through the cemetery, and he too did not realise there was a freshly dug grave. In the darkness of the night, the second man fell into the same open grave, and did not notice the first man fast asleep in the corner.

The second man also yelled and screamed, but eventually he worked out that there was no way out. He was starting to panic! Imagine being trapped in a grave at night! He had to admit he had reached a dead end.

And then he felt a hand on his shoulder. And he heard a voice booming from behind: *"You'll never get out of here!"*

When he felt that hand—when he heard that voice—he shot out of that grave like a rocket! Suddenly he had the strength to do what he could not do before! He shot out of the grave and ran the four-minute mile as he scampered all the way home. He had been facing a dead end, but something new had entered into his life, and suddenly his dead end was not trapping him in any longer. Something new came into his life, and his dead end was smashed and had become a freeway!

I don't know what "dead ends" you are facing in your life. There can be so many situations where it looks as if you're "hemmed in" and there's no way out.

Perhaps you're at school and you know no matter how hard you study—you'll never really catch up… dead end! Maybe you know you can never meet your parents' expectations… dead end! Perhaps everything is going well for you. You're successful, and you're on top of everything. But deep inside there's an emptiness which achievement, money, or sex just don't seem to satisfy… dead end! Or it might be simply that you want to follow

> You want to follow God, but you always let him down…

God, but you always let him down. No matter how
hard you try to be a faithful Christian—you just can't
do it… dead end!

Here's the good news: no matter what situation you
are in, God has another move up his sleeve. God is
more powerful than any of the dead ends in your
life—and there is a real hope and a real purpose to
where you are heading. And just as that man in the
graveyard thought there was no way forward… just as he
discovered that when a new factor entered his situation he had
the power to accomplish things that he could never do before… the good
news is that Jesus can enter your life and change it forever—to give you real
hope and a real purpose to everything you do.

WHAT WE WERE LIKE – SPIRITUALLY DEAD!

Ephesians 2:1-3

*As for you, you were dead in your transgressions and sins, in
which you used to live when you followed the ways of this world
and of the ruler of the kingdom of the air, the spirit who is now
at work in those who are disobedient. All of us also lived among
them at one time, gratifying the cravings of our sinful nature
and following its desires and thoughts. Like the rest, we were by
nature objects of wrath.*

If you're not yet a genuine Christian, God describes you as being
spiritually dead. That's a very strong description. And yet it is a true
description. It describes everyone who has not been made alive by Jesus. It
described me before I became a Christian.

> *"But what do you mean—spiritually dead?"*

Imagine you have a bunch of freshly-cut flowers. You have cut them from
your garden, and brought them inside the house and placed them in a vase
of water. Here's the question: are those flowers alive or dead? They certainly
look alive—they're tall and colourful with a beautiful fragrance—but I want
to suggest that they are dead. They have been cut off from their source of

life—so even though they look alive, in fact they are dead. And if you leave them in that vase for long enough, you will see that they really are dead!

In the same way, when we cut ourselves off from Jesus—our source of spiritual life—we are in fact spiritually dead. We might look alive—we might live busy and active lives… we might stand tall and proud and arrayed in beautiful colours… but if we've been cut off from the source of our spiritual life, we are spiritually dead. And if you leave us long enough, you will see that we are indeed spiritually dead.

Can a corpse bring themselves back to life?

Notice carefully that God describes us as being spiritually **dead**—not spiritually **sick**. There is a huge difference between the two! When a person is sick, we call the doctor. When a person is dead, we call the undertaker. When a person is sick, we give them the right medicine so that they might get better. If a person is dead, there is no medicine in the world that will do them any good!

Now imagine there is a dead body lying on the ground in front of you. Any life that they had has been snuffed out hours ago. They are dead—they are a corpse. Here's the question: *"what can a dead person do to bring themselves back to life?"* The answer is nothing! There's no use giving them a drink of water. It will not work. Even if we have some magic elixir that can bring people back to life, and we put the bottle right next to them and say: *"Drink it! Go on, drink it!"*—no matter how long we exhort, encourage or cajole them, **there is nothing a physically dead person can do to bring themselves back to life.**

So—what can someone who is spiritually dead do to give themselves eternal life? Nothing. If we are spiritually dead, there is nothing we can do. We cannot do one thing that will make God like us and accept us.

Ephesians 2:4-5

But because of his great love for us, God, who is rich in mercy, made us alive with Christ even when we were dead in transgressions—it is by grace you have been saved...

What we couldn't do for ourselves, God did for us.

We were deserving God's punishment—but Jesus came and completely took the punishment for those who are his. We could not perfectly obey our heavenly Father—but Jesus as our representative lived a life of perfect obedience. We could not have victory over sin—but Jesus completely conquered sin by his death on the cross. We could not avoid the terror of death—but Jesus came and smashed the power of death in his resurrection. We could never be good enough to become God's children—but Jesus, as the perfect Son, shares his sonship with us. We could never hope to gain eternal life—but Jesus, as the risen King, gives us life forever with the Father.

What we could not do for ourselves, God has done for us.

That's what the Bible means by: *"It is by grace you have been saved."*

1. What is grace?

Grace is when you give someone a gift, or do someone a favour, when they do not deserve it. Grace is trying to save the life of a man who has been injured while blowing up your car. Grace is visiting in prison the person who has molested your best friend. Grace is being kind to the person who is continually hurting you.

You do something for someone that they do not deserve. That's grace. That is what God does for you. He has given you something that you do not deserve. He has sent his son Jesus to die for people who were his enemies. Jesus gets what we deserve, and we get what Jesus deserves.

That's grace. G-R-A-C-E:

- **G**od's
- **R**iches
- **A**t
- **C**hrist's
- **E**xpense

God has completely done for us what we didn't deserve, and what we had no hope of doing for ourselves. He has accomplished total victory over the devil, and he gives to us eternal life with him as a free, undeserved gift. He gives us the gift of being his sons and daughters. He gives us a totally transformed life.

That's what the Bible means when it says: *"It is by grace you have been saved."*

2. What is faith?

So how are we meant to respond to this great act of mercy by God?

> **Ephesians 2:8**
> *For it is by grace you have been saved—through faith.*

When someone gives you a present, how do you respond? I guess it depends how much you trust them! Generally, you say "thank you" and you take their gift, unwrap it, and make it your own and enjoy it. That's faith!

Take it, unwrap it, make it yours, enjoy it.

Because at that particular point, you are trusting that person that the gift they are giving you will be good for you. You are trusting them that what they have placed in your hands is not a time bomb which is about to destroy your life. You are trusting them that the gift they are giving you is not a snake that is going to jump out and poison you.

Because you trust them that the gift they are giving you will be good for you, you thank them for it, take it, unwrap it, make it yours and enjoy it. That's faith.

So, how should you respond to the free gift of eternal life which God gives? You need to have faith in God to know that what he is giving you will be good for you. So that you can thank him for his gift, take it, unwrap it, make it yours and enjoy it.

That's faith. F-A-I-T-H:

- **F**orsaking
- **A**ll
- **I**
- **T**rust
- **H**im

You know, some people don't trust God. They don't have faith that what God is giving them will be good for them. They somehow think that if they accept what God offers, their life will be wrecked. That God is out to cheat them, to con them, to destroy them.

And if you don't have faith in God at that point, then you won't trust him that his gift is a good gift. You won't take his gift. You won't unwrap it and enjoy it. You'll reject it—you'll send it back.

Can you see the outrageous and extraordinary thing that God has already done for us?

> ### Ephesians 2: 4-9
> But because of his great love for us, God, who is rich in mercy, made us alive with Christ even when we were dead in transgressions—it is by grace you have been saved.
>
> And God raised us up with Christ and seated us with him in the heavenly realms in Christ Jesus, in order that in the coming ages he might show the incomparable riches of his grace, expressed in his kindness to us in Christ Jesus.
>
> For it is by grace you have been saved, through faith—and this not from yourselves, it is the gift of God—not by works, so that no-one can boast.

But what if I've never taken that first step? What am I meant to do?

Next chapter!

How do I start?

*This whole book has been about being **totally transformed**. We've looked at the new life that God calls you to once he makes you a new person in Jesus. We've looked at...*

- Totally transformed speech
- Totally transformed fun
- Totally transformed submission
- Totally transformed sex
- Totally transformed mission

You might be reading all this and thinking to yourself:

> *"I don't know I've even taken the first step. I keep trying to live this new life, but nothing's working. I'm not even sure that I'm really a Christian."*

Maybe you've haven't taken that first step. Maybe you want to live for Jesus but you've never taken that step of trusting him. Maybe you've never accepted that free gift of forgiveness that Jesus is offering. You might have looked at God's gift—you might have admired God's gift—but maybe you've never taken it, unwrapped it, and made it yours.

Perhaps today is the day for you to start a totally transformed life. Let's check back over these verses in Ephesians Chapter 2, so you'll see more clearly the step that God wants you to make.

BY OURSELVES WE ARE DEAD

Ephesians 2:1
You were dead in your transgressions and sins…

By our own efforts we can never make it to God. Our sins have cut us off from eternal life. That means we are all spiritually dead.

BY OURSELVES WE DESERVE GOD'S JUDGMENT

Ephesians 2:3

… gratifying the cravings of our sinful nature and following its desires and thoughts. Like the rest, we were by nature objects of wrath.

By our own efforts, we just end up pleasing ourselves. We rebel against God—which means we deserve his judgment. This spells eternal death.

BUT GOD CAN MAKE US ALIVE WITH JESUS!

Ephesians 2:4-5

But because of his great love for us, God, who is rich in mercy, made us alive with Christ even when we were dead in transgressions—it is by grace you have been saved.

God does for us what we could not do for ourselves. He loves us so much that he sent his Son Jesus to die for our sins. He forgives all our sins and gives us eternal life.

And we don't deserve that at all—which is why it is called God's **grace.**

GOD HAS TAKEN US TO HEAVEN WITH JESUS

Ephesians 2:6

And God raised us up with Christ and seated us with him in the heavenly realms in Christ Jesus.

Jesus did not stay dead, but rose triumphantly from the grave, and then ascended back to heaven. When you join up with Jesus, he guarantees to take you to heaven with him. That means life with him— **forever!**

WE MUST RECEIVE THIS GIFT BY FAITH

Ephesians 2:8

For it is by grace you have been saved, through faith—and this not from yourselves, it is the gift of God—not by works, so that no one can boast.

What God offers us by **grace,** we must receive by **faith.** Faith means that we admit that we can't get eternal life by ourselves, but we trust God enough to receive the gift he is offering us. We trust God enough to submit our whole life to him.

THEN GOD GIVES US A TOTALLY TRANSFORMED LIFE

Ephesians 2:10

For we are God's workmanship, created in Christ Jesus to do good works, which God prepared in advance for us to do.

There's a whole stack of **good works** that God has now created us to do! There is a brand new life he wants us to live—where our speech, our fun, our submission, our sex, our mission—our whole life—is **totally transformed!**

SO HOW DO I TAKE THAT FIRST STEP?

Have you ever taken that first step of saying **"yes"** to Jesus? Have you given up trying to make it under your own strength? Do you realise that Jesus died to forgive you and rose to give you new life—and that he offers all this to you as a gift? And all you need to do is say **"yes"**—say **"yes"** with your heart, and **"yes"** with your whole life.

If you've never taken that step, and you know that you are ready to take it, then take a moment now and commit your life to Jesus. Not just for today… not just for a while… but **for eternity.**

You can use your own words… or use the following prayer if it helps you:

Dear God,
I admit that I keep doing the wrong thing. I don't deserve your friendship. I need your help.

I believe that Jesus died for me so that I am forgiven. I believe that Jesus rose for me so that I have eternal life. Please take away all my sin, and help me live this brand new life.

I commit my life to following you. Please take over my life and start running it your way. I want to live the rest of my days

obeying you no matter what. Father God, please help me to
live a totally transformed life.   Amen.

If you have taken that step, and you genuinely meant it—if you spoke to God from your heart, and you truly want to serve him all your days—then here is the most well-known promise in the whole Bible—and it now applies to you:

John 3:16
For God so loved the world that he gave his one and only Son,
that whoever believes in him shall not perish but have eternal life.

That is an iron-clad guarantee from God. Whenever you **believe** in him—that is, place your whole trust in what Jesus has done for you by dying and rising—then God guarantees you two things:

- You will not perish (in hell)
- You have eternal life (in God's new creation)

If you have genuinely given your life to Jesus, then those promises apply to you now. God has already **totally transformed** you. He is now calling on you to live a **totally transformed** life.

WHAT NOW?

The most important thing now is to **keep on growing.** If you stand still as a Christian, you will probably end up going backwards. Here are three simple keys to keep you growing strong. Start these three things today—and determine you will never give them up.

1. Link up with God

God has so many things to teach you—and he's written them in his book, the Bible. It's really important that you link up with God by reading part of his word every day. That's how God will speak to you. And don't forget—it's a two-way conversation so make sure you talk with God in prayer every day.

If you don't have a Bible, try and get one from the same place you got this book. Did someone give you this book? Well, go back and ask them if they can

help you with a Bible. Did you buy this book at a store? Well, go back to the store and ask to see their Bibles. If you have a friend who's a Christian, they will certainly help you. Or contact the publisher of this book!

2. Link up with God's people

Living as a Christian is never meant to be a solo sport—it is a team sport! It is **vital** that you link up with some other Christians to learn and grow. If you already go to a church or Christian youth group, then make sure that you tell your friends there the step that you have made. If you know any Christians, go along with them to their church. There might even be a Christian group at your school, uni or workplace. But whatever you do, please don't try to live as a Christian by yourself. God has supplied a whole gang of fellow Christians to help you learn and grow.

3. Bring others with you

If you've discovered some great new things about Jesus—then don't keep them to yourself! Go and help some of your friends to enjoy the **totally transformed** life that you have just started. Wouldn't it be a thrill if you were able to help some of your friends to become Christians too? Don't wait until next week—start inviting people today!

If you belong to Jesus, then God has already recreated you to be a **totally transformed** person. He is now calling on you to live a **totally transformed** life. The adventure starts now!

Are you ready to start those transformations that God has in mind for you?

Want to read more?

Hope you've enjoyed reading this book. If so, you might like to get hold of the Bible study that goes with it, or dig into another book. Take a look at one of these websites and see what's on offer to help you live a Totally Transformed life.

UK	www.thegoodbook.co.uk
USA	www.thegoodbook.com
Australia:	www.hawkinsministry.com
	www.thegoodbook.com.au
New Zealand	www.thegoodbook.co.nz